BUSINESS ENTREPRENEURSHIP BEYOND THE 9 TO 5

For Those Starting Out or Starting Over

TAYLOR DANIELS

Copyright © 2022 Taylor Daniels

All rights reserved.

No part of this publication may be reproduced, distributed or transmitted in any form or by any means, including photocopying, recording or other electronic or mechanical methods, without the prior written permission of the publisher, except in the case of brief quotations, reviews and other noncommercial uses permitted by copyright law.

Contents

Introduction..7

Chapter 1. What is a business?........................9
- Business sizes..............................12

Chapter 2. Meaning of entrepreneur....................15
- The characteristics of entrepreneurship..........17
- Importance of entrepreneurship..............20
- The advantages of being an entrepreneur.......24
- The disadvantages of being an entrepreneur.....26

Chapter 3. What is entrepreneurship, and who is an entrepreneur?..........................29
- Entrepreneurial qualities....................30
- Some famous entrepreneurs.................32
- 5 Types of entrepreneurs....................35

Chapter 4. An entrepreneur working 9-5...............41
- Start your business around your 9-to-5 job......45
- How to start a business while working.........50

Chapter 5. Seven compelling reasons to start a business......55
- How to start a small business 57
- How to start a business from scratch with (almost) no money 68
- Development of excellent business concepts.....73

Chapter 6. Define and research your target market.........77
- Different types of business structures 81
- Describe what your company is/does............85
- How to be a successful business owner.........86

Chapter 7. Marketing and growth.......................93
- Ways to become a more successful entrepreneur...95
- There are a few ways you can fund your business: 101

Chapter 8. Funding options to raise startup capital for your business 107
- The best small businesses to invest in 114
- Best business idea to make money?...........118
- Other business ideas 130

Chapter 9. How to advance your career.................133
- What should you do after landing the big job?..135
- There are things you can do today to improve your career......................138
- Career advancement opportunities 141
- Why is career advancement important? 141

- How to overcome career advancement challenges 142
- How to advance in your career 144
- When is it best to start your business? 148

Conclusion 149

INTRODUCTION

The Concept of Entrepreneurship

In the past, there was no forthright definition of an entrepreneur. For centuries, scholars ignored entrepreneurship, particularly those in economics who argued that there was no place for taking risks in business. In their opinion, companies could only thrive in situations with perfect information.

Entrepreneurship is the ability and readiness to develop, organize, and run a business enterprise, along with any of its uncertainties, to make a profit. The most prominent example of entrepreneurship is the starting of new businesses.

In economics, entrepreneurship connected with land, labor, natural resources, and capital can generate a profit. The entrepreneurial vision is by discovery and risk-taking and is an indispensable part of a nation's capacity to succeed in an ever-changing and more competitive global marketplace.

Chapter 1

WHAT IS A BUSINESS?

"Business" refers to an organization or enterprising entity engaged in commercial, industrial, or professional activities. The purpose of a business is to organize some economic production (of goods or services). Businesses can be for-profit entities or non-profit organizations fulfilling a charitable mission or furthering a social cause. Businesses range in scale and scope from sole proprietorships to large international corporations.

The business also refers to the efforts and activities undertaken by individuals to produce and sell goods and services for profit.

Key Takeaway: A business is an organization or enterprising entity engaged in commercial, industrial, or professional activities. Businesses can be for-profit entities or non-profit organizations.

Business types range from limited liability companies to sole proprietorships, corporations, and partnerships.

Some businesses are run as small operations in a single industry, while others are large operations that are spread across many industries around the world.

Apple and Walmart are two examples of well-known, successful businesses.

UNDERSTANDING BUSINESS

The term "business" often refers to an entity that operates for commercial, industrial, or professional reasons. The concept begins with an idea and a name.

Extensive market research may be required to determine how feasible it is to turn the idea into a business.

A business often requires a business plan before operations begin. A business plan is a formal document that outlines the company's goals and objectives and lists the strategies and plans to achieve these goals and objectives. Business plans are essential when you want to borrow capital to begin operations.

Determining the business's legal structure is an essential factor since business owners may need to secure permits and licenses and follow registration requirements to begin legal operations. Corporations are legal in many countries, meaning the business can own property, take on debt, and be sued in court.

Most businesses, also known as for-profit enterprises, exist to make a profit. However, some companies that have a goal of advancing a particular cause without profit are referred to as not-for-profit or nonprofit. These organizations include charitable, arts, culture, educational, recreational, political, advocacy, or social service organizations.

Business activities often include the sale and purchase of goods and services. Business activity can occur anywhere, on a physical storefront, online, or on the roadside. Anyone conducting business with financial earnings must report this income to the Internal Revenue Service (IRS).

BUSINESS TYPES

There are many ways to organize a business, and there are various legal and tax structures that correspond with these. Among others, companies are commonly classified and generally structured as follows:

1. Sole proprietorships: As the name suggests, a sole proprietorship is owned and operated by a single person. There is no legal separation between the Business and the owner, which means the tax and legal liabilities of the business are the responsibility of the owner.
2. Partnerships: A partnership is a business relationship formed by two or more individuals who do business together. Each partner contributes resources and money to the company and shares in the profits and losses of the business. The shared profits and losses are recorded on each partner's tax return.

3. Corporations: A corporation is a business in which a group of people acts as a single entity. Owners are commonly referred to as shareholders who exchange consideration for the corporation's common stock. Incorporating a business releases owners from the financial liability of business obligations. Corporations come with unfavorable taxation rules for the owners of businesses.
4. Limited liability companies (LLCs): This is a relatively new business structure and was first available in Wyoming in 1977 and in other states in the 1990s. A limited liability company combines the pass-through taxation benefits of a partnership with the limited liability benefits of a corporation.

BUSINESS SIZES

1. Small Businesses

Small owner-operated companies are called "small businesses." These companies are commonly overseen by one person or a small group with fewer than 100 employees. They include family restaurants, home-based companies, clothing, books, publishing companies, and small manufacturers. As of 2021, 32.5 million small businesses with 61.2 million employees were operating in the United States.

Businesses that meet the standards of the SBA can qualify for loans, grants, and "small business set-asides" contracts where the federal government limits competition to help small businesses compete for and win federal contracts.

2. Mid-Sized Businesses

There is no definitive specification in the U.S. to define a mid-sized or medium-sized company. However, when large U.S. cities such as Philadelphia, Baltimore, and Boston evaluate the landscape of operating businesses, a medium-sized company is defined as one with 100 to 499 employees or $10 million to less than $50 million in annual gross sales.

3. Large Corporations

Large businesses commonly have over 1,000 employees and garner $50 million or more in gross receipts. They may issue corporate stock to finance operations as a publicly traded company.

Large enterprises may be based in one country but have international operations. They are often organized by departments, such as human resources, finance, marketing, sales, and research and development. Unlike small and mid-sized enterprises, owned by a person or group of people, large organizations often separate their tax burden from their owners, who usually do not manage their companies; instead, an elected board of directors enacts most business decisions.

Chapter 2

MEANING OF ENTREPRENEUR

The entrepreneur is defined as someone who has the ability and desires to establish, administer and succeed in a startup venture, along with the risk entitled to it, to make profits. The best example of entrepreneurship is the starting of a new business venture. Entrepreneurs are often known as a source of new ideas or innovators and bring new ideas to the market by replacing old with new inventions.

It can be categorized from small or home businesses to multinational companies. In economics, the profits that an entrepreneur makes are with a combination of land, natural resources, labor, and capital.

In a nutshell, anyone who has the will and determination to start a new company and deal with all the risks that go with it can become an entrepreneur.

What Are The Four Types Of Entrepreneurship? It has the following types:

➢ **Small Business Entrepreneurship-**

These businesses include hairdressers, grocery stores, travel agents, consultants, carpenters, plumbers, electricians, etc. These people run or own a business and hire family members or local employees. For them, the profit would be able to feed their family and not make a 100 million business or take over an industry. They fund their business by taking small business loans or loans from friends and family.

➢ **Scalable Startup Entrepreneurship-**

This start-up entrepreneur starts a business knowing that their vision can change the world. They attract investors who think and encourage people who think outside the box. The research focuses on scalable businesses and experimental models, so they hire the best and the brightest employees. They require more venture capital to fuel and back their projects or businesses.

➢ **Large Company Entrepreneurship-**

These giant companies have a defined life cycle. Most of these companies grow and are sustained by offering new and innovative products that revolve around their main products. The change in technology, customer preferences, new competition, etc., builds pressure on large companies to create an innovative product and sell it to a new set of customers in the new market. To cope with the rapid technological changes, existing organizations either buy innovative enterprises or attempt to construct the product internally.

> ➤ Social Entrepreneurship-

This type of entrepreneurship focuses on producing products and services that resolve social needs and problems. Their only motto and goal are to work for society and not make any profits.

THE CHARACTERISTICS OF ENTREPRENEURSHIP

Not all entrepreneurs are thriving; there are definite characteristics that make entrepreneurship successful. Here are a few notes below:

> ➤ The ability to take a risk

Starting any new venture involves a considerable amount of failure risk. Therefore, an entrepreneur needs to be courageous and able to evaluate and take risks, which is an essential part of being an entrepreneur. Successful entrepreneurs are comfortable with encountering some level of risk to reap the rewards of their efforts. However, their risk tolerance is tightly related to their mitigating actions.

INNOVATION

It should be highly innovative to generate new ideas, start a company, and earn profits. Change can be the launching of a new product that is new to the market or a process that does the same thing but more efficiently and economically. Innovation is a characteristic some, but not all, entrepreneurs possess. Fortunately, it's a type of strategic mindset that can be developed. By developing your strategic thinking skills, you can be well-equipped to spot innovative opportunities and position your venture Visionary and leadership qualities

To be successful, an entrepreneur should have a clear vision of his new venture. However, to turn the idea into reality, a lot of resources and employees are required. Here, leadership quality is paramount because leaders impart and guide their employees toward the right path of success.

OPEN-MINDED

In a business, every circumstance can be an opportunity used for the company's benefit. For example, Paytm recognized the gravity of demonetization and Acknowledged the need for online transactions would be more significant, so it utilized the situation and expanded massively during this time.

FLEXIBLE

An entrepreneur should be flexible and open to change according to the situation. A businessperson should be ready to embrace change in a product or service as and when needed. Understand your product.

A company owner should know the product offerings and be aware of the latest trends in the market. It is essential to understand if the available product or service meets the current market's demands or whether it is time to tweak it a little. Being able to be accountable and then alter as needed is a vital part of entrepreneurship.

Adaptability

The nature of business is ever-changing. Entrepreneurship is an iterative process, and new challenges and opportunities present themselves at every turn. It's nearly impossible to be prepared for every scenario, but successful business leaders must be adaptable. These characteristics are especially true for entrepreneurs who need to evaluate situations and remain flexible to ensure their business keeps moving forward, no matter what unexpected changes occur.

Team Building

A great entrepreneur is aware of their strengths and weaknesses. Rather than letting shortcomings hold them back, they build well-rounded teams that complement their abilities.

In many cases, it's the entrepreneurial team, rather than an individual, that drives a venture toward success. When starting your own business, it's critical to surround yourself with teammates who have complementary talents and contribute to a common goal.

Persistence

While many successful entrepreneurs are comfortable with the possibility of failing, it doesn't mean they give up easily. Rather, they see failure as an opportunity to learn and grow.

Throughout the entrepreneurial process, many hypotheses turn out wrong, and some ventures fail altogether. Part of what makes an entrepreneur successful is their willingness to learn from mistakes, continue to ask questions and persist until they reach their goal.

Long-Term Focus

Finally, most people think of entrepreneurship as the process of starting a business. While the early stages of launching a venture are critical to its success, the process doesn't end once the business is operational. Starting a business is easy, but hard to grow a sustainable and substantial one. Some of the most significant opportunities in history were well after a venture had launched.

Entrepreneurship is a long-term endeavor, and entrepreneurs must focus on the process from beginning to end to ensure long-term success.

IMPORTANCE OF ENTREPRENEURSHIP

In entrepreneurship, unutilized resources, labor, and capital are the most efficient. Entrepreneurs take on risks in the hopes of making a profit, or in the case of social entrepreneurship, of solving a problem facing communities. So, the significance of entrepreneurs and the role of entrepreneurship go beyond the business world. The importance of entrepreneurship is so broad that it's pretty tough to explain all the aspects of it in a short blog post. However, I would like to shed some light on the importance and role of entrepreneurship in economic development and society.

1. Entrepreneurship Accelerates Economic Growth.

Entrepreneurs are essential to market economies because they can act as the wheels of the country's economic growth.

By creating new products and services, they stimulate new employment, which ultimately results in the acceleration of economic development. Therefore, public policy encouraging and supporting entrepreneurship should be considered essential for economic growth.

Entrepreneurship creates a large number of new jobs and opportunities. Entrepreneurship creates many entry-level jobs to turn unskilled job holders into skilled ones. It also prepares and provides experienced workers for large industries. The increase in the total employment of a country largely depends on the rise of entrepreneurship. So the role of entrepreneurship in creating new job opportunities is enormous.

By bringing innovation to every aspect of business, entrepreneurial ventures enhance production, utilizing the existing resources effectively. Entrepreneurs develop new markets by introducing new and improved products, services, and technology. Thus, they help generate new wealth and increase national income. So the government can offer the citizens more federal benefits.

◻ Entrepreneurship Promotes Innovation

Through the proper practices of research and development, entrepreneurs bring innovation that opens the door to new ventures, markets, products, and technology. Entrepreneurs have a role in solving problems that existing products and technology have not yet solved. So, by producing new products and services or bringing innovation to existing Products and services, and entrepreneurship have the potential to improve people's lives.

◻ Entrepreneurship can promote social change.

Entrepreneurs change or break the traditions or cultures of society and reduce the dependency on obsolete methods, systems, and technologies. Entrepreneurs are the pioneers of introducing new technologies and techniques that ultimately bring changes to the community. These changes are associated with improved lifestyles, generous thinking, better morale, and higher economic choice. In this way, social changes gradually impact national and global changes. The importance of social networking services and entrepreneurship must be respected.

◻ Entrepreneurship promotes research and industrial development.

Along with producing new business ideas and thinking outside the box, entrepreneurs also encourage research and development.

They cultivate their ideas, shape them into a new form, and turn them into successful business endeavors.

Entrepreneurs are special people. They are constantly working to discover new ideas and improve existing ones. However, their influence extends beyond their businesses and ventures; when an entrepreneur creates a new product, service, or thought, others frequently follow (and sometimes refine the ideas).

Innovation and industry are accelerated through the combined action of entrepreneurs. They can motivate, share ideas and inspiration, and work together to establish new initiatives. The change to the existing

Industrial climate opens doors for others at the same time. Therefore, we see that the importance of entrepreneurship to the economy is multi-functional.

☐ Entrepreneurship Develops and Improves Existing Enterprises.

We often think of entrepreneurs as inventing new products and ideas, but they also impact existing businesses. Since entrepreneurs think differently, they can come up with innovative ways to expand and develop their existing enterprises. For example, modernizing production processes, implementing new technology in the overall distribution and marketing processes, and helping existing enterprises to utilize existing resources in more efficient ways are some of the actions that exist.

Supporting and promoting entrepreneurship can positively impact the country's economy and even existing businesses, and social entrepreneurship increases the likelihood of finding innovative solutions to social challenges faced by communities around the world.

THE ADVANTAGES OF BEING AN ENTREPRENEUR

A flexible schedule—both in terms of when and where you work:

One of the best things and most significant advantages of being an entrepreneur is that you can work from home, work from the office (if you have one), and work from virtually any destination with a great view and a glass of wine in your hand!

You can also choose when you work. If you want to stay up late, stay up late. If you're going to get up early, get up early. The flexibility of having your own business; remains, in my opinion, one of the best advantages of being an entrepreneur. It is hard to come by this flexibility in any other job!

1. You learn a lot:

   Not just about your field but about accounting, marketing, public speaking, website design, search engine optimization, how to delegate, how to take risks, how to be more creative, and think about problems in other ways. And, importantly, how to fail, how to be rejected, and how to get back up on your feet anyway.

I have always been attracted to business because it seems like a unique and diversified set of skills is required, such as setting up a website, marketing, getting appointments with clients, and delegation.

This is one of the advantages of being an entrepreneur that I overlooked initially. I figured I knew what I was doing and that even if I didn't, I could figure it out without falling too many times. But I was wrong. And very grateful for it.

2. It's exciting and fulfilling:

It is exciting to build something from the ground up. Especially when you love what you do, it is such an incredible feeling to make something out of nothing. And it is so much fun to hire extraordinary people to work for the company. And to have amazing clients, many of whom are not only paying customers but also friends!

The ups and downs are never-ending. It is never dull. It is my third year, and I still have a roller-coaster feeling when I start a new project or when we fulfill a new idea.

3. The salary makes sense:

When you make money, you get paid more. It is not an arbitrary number that you are each year. And you don't have to wait for someone to give you A raise. You get to keep the profits. You pay the expenses. And if you are doing it right, this will end up being a good deal.

4. You are a leader:

Being a leader was my favorite part of the increased confidence. People say, "you have a brilliant business model," and all sorts of compliments are very nice. And to be honest, one I am not sure I have truly earned. But it is a very nice side benefit!

THE DISADVANTAGES OF BEING AN ENTREPRENEUR

You wear a lot of hats. You are not just the owner of the company. You are the CEO, secretary, website designer, accountant, head of marketing, and janitor. That is until you can afford to delegate this to contractors and employees. And then you take on the title of "employer," which, true, replaces some of these other titles but also brings a whole new set of benefits and challenges to the table.

1. You are always at work.

> You can indeed work from anywhere and at any time. But really, that is because you are working everywhere at all times! I have heard entrepreneurs "beat 9-5 to work 9-9." There is some truth to that. You are always on call and always doing something for the company. Even now, I am writing this from a lovely suite in Bay City overlooking the water at 6:00 AM in my hotel-bathroom-counter-converted-into-makeshift-desk so that I do not wake my spouse! If you love what you do, then it does not seem so bad! (In the end, I think that is how entrepreneurs survive—believing in their vision and loving their work!)

17 posted on Work-life balance becomes tricky and is sometimes non-existent.

Work-life balance becomes tricky. It is hard to draw a line between "work" and "life" when you work from home. When your office and your living space are the same, your phone is your work phone (even if you have a work phone)—the same with a personal email. And, of course, personal time (remember, you're always on call). It doesn't mean you can't place limits on work-life balance. Or draw a line. Or do not check your e-mail after 7:00. Or do not work on Sunday mornings. And it is not to say it is not a challenge for other professions. However, it does seem to be for entrepreneurs.

2. A non-regular paycheck can be scary.

If your company doesn't make money, you don't make money. So, in some ways, while the salary is "rational" – you get what you put in – in other ways, it is not. Because you can work 50 hours a week and make nothing, this is both liberating and terrifying.

3. You will feel a new kind of stress.

Entrepreneurial ventures can bring about a new kind of stress. Instead of being an employee, you are responsible for all decisions. If you fail or succeed, customers, vendors, employees, and others are looking at you. So just as you can stand out as a "leader" (Advantage 5 above), you can also be looked at as a fool.

TAYLOR DANIELS

Stress can amplify if you do not have a consistent income. Or if you don't have health insurance. Or if you don't feel your self-employment is exceptionally "secure."

Chapter 3

WHAT IS ENTREPRENEURSHIP, AND WHO IS AN ENTREPRENEUR?

We often hear that so-and-so is an entrepreneur who has started their own business. It is also the case that when we hear the term "entrepreneur," we tend to associate it with a person who has or is starting their ventures, or in other words, striking it on their own. The formal definition of entrepreneurship is starting a business or an organization for profit or social needs. We have used the phrase for profit or social needs to separate commercial entrepreneurship from social and charitable entrepreneurship. After defining entrepreneurship, it is time to determine who an entrepreneur is and what they do.

An Entrepreneur is someone who develops a business model, acquires the necessary physical and human capital to start a new venture, operationalizes it, and is responsible for its success or failure. The emphasis on "responsible for success or failure" is essential because the entrepreneur differs from the professional manager in that the former either invests their resources or raises capital from external sources and thus bears the blame for failure as well as reaps the rewards in case of success, whereas the latter, or professional manager, does the job and the work assigned to them for a monetary consideration other words, the entrepreneur is the risk-taker and an innovator addition to being a creator of new enterprise's. In contrast, the professional manager is simply the executor.

ENTREPRENEURIAL QUALITIES

Moving to the skills and capabilities that an entrepreneur needs to have, first and foremost, they have to be an innovator with a game-changing idea or a potentially new concept that can succeed in the crowded marketplace. It is important to note that investors typically invest in ideas and concepts that they believe will generate adequate returns on their capital and investments; thus, the entrepreneur must have a truly innovative idea for a new venture.

1. Leadership Qualities

   Apart from this, the entrepreneur needs to have excellent organizational and people management skills as they have to build the organization or the venture from scratch and have to bond with their employees and vibe well with the other stakeholders to ensure the venture's success. Further, the entrepreneur needs to be a leader who can inspire their employees and be a visionary and a person with a sense of mission. The entrepreneur must motivate and drive the venture. Meaning that leadership, values, team-building skills, and managerial abilities are the essential skills and attributes that an entrepreneur needs to have.

2. Creative Destruction and Entrepreneurship

We often hear the term "creative destruction" being spoken about when discussing how some companies fade away. In contrast, others succeed and maintain their leadership position in the marketplace. Creative destruction refers to the replacement of inferior products and companies by more efficient, innovative, and creative ones, wherein the capitalist market-based ecosystem ensures that only the best and brightest survive. In contrast, others are blown away by the gales of creative destruction. In other words, entrepreneurs with game-changing ideas and the skills and attributes that are needed to succeed, ensure that their products, brands, and ventures take market share away from existing companies that are either not creating value or are simply inefficient and stuck in a time warp wherein they cannot see the writing on the wall. Therefore, this process of destroying the old and the weak through newer and creative ideas is called "creative destruction," which entrepreneurs often do when they launch a new venture.

3. An Entrepreneur is a Risk-Taker

We have discussed what entrepreneurship is and the skills and attributes needed by entrepreneurs, along with how they engage and indulge in creative destruction. It does not mean that all entrepreneurs are successful, as the fact that they can become victims of creative destruction, as well as due to a lack of other traits, means that a majority of new ventures do not survive past the one-year mark of their existence. When ventures fail, the obvious question is who takes the blame for the failure and whose money is lost. The answer is that the entrepreneur either puts in their own money or raises capital from angel investors and venture capitalists, which means that if the venture goes belly up, the entrepreneur and the investors lose money.

Note that, as mentioned earlier, the employees and the professional managers lose their jobs, and unless they are partners in the venture, their money is not at stake. Therefore, this means that the entrepreneur is the risk-taker in the experience, which means that the success or failure of the firm reflects on the entrepreneur.

SOME FAMOUS ENTREPRENEURS

Given this basic introduction to entrepreneurship, we can now turn to some famous examples of entrepreneurs who have succeeded despite heavy odds because they had game-changing ideas and, more importantly, they also had the necessary traits and skills that would make them legendary. For instance, the founder of Microsoft, Bill Gates, and the late Steve Jobs, the founder of

Apple, were college dropouts. However, their eventual success meant that they had not only genuinely innovative ideas, but they were also ready to strike it out for the long term and hang on when the going got tough. Even the founder of Facebook, Mark Zuckerberg, and Google's Larry Paige and Sergey Brian, can be considered genuinely revolutionary entrepreneurs. What all these legends have in common is that they had the vision and the sense of mission that they were going to change the world, and with hard work, perseverance, and a nurturing ecosystem, they were able to self-actualize themselves.

Entrepreneurship Needs a Nurturing Ecosystem

Finally, note the use of the term "nurturing ecosystem. Meaning that just as entrepreneurs cannot succeed if they lack the necessary attributes, they cannot grow if they live in an environment or a country that does not encourage risk or tolerate failure and, more importantly, is unable to provide them with the monetary and human capital needed for success. The United States remains the preeminent country for entrepreneurship as it has the required ecosystem for these entrepreneurs to succeed. In contrast, in many countries, it is often impossible or difficult to find funding, work through red tape, and ensure that environmental factors do not inhibit entrepreneurship.

SKILLS FOR A SUCCESSFUL ENTREPRENEUR

Entrepreneurs need a unique set of skills to be successful, including:

➢ Time Management Skills

Many entrepreneurs oversee multiple aspects of their business. From project management to design to development, entrepreneurs often handle several tasks simultaneously and require strong time management skills to finish each duty.

➢ Networking Skills

An effective networker is one of the best ways to grow your business opportunities, find high-quality employees, and secure partnerships. Plus, networking helps advertise your business, which is key to increasing awareness and revenue. Promoting and securing sales is an integral part of being an entrepreneur. From knowing which sales channels to utilize to implementing sales funnels, sales skills help entrepreneurs become profitable.

➢ Communication Skills

Entrepreneurs often must communicate with contractors, employees, clients, investors, and partners. Both written and verbal communication skills are often necessary for entrepreneurs.

➢ Finance Skills

Entrepreneurs are often responsible for all the financial aspects of their businesses. Meaning entrepreneurs must possess strong financial skills, including financial reporting, financial analysis, and risk management skills.

5 TYPES OF ENTREPRENEURS

Understanding The Unique Differences

Entrepreneurs turn bold ideas into reality. They create jobs and contribute to the economy, but there are different types of entrepreneurs, and each tends to choose their path based on their personality, abilities, and surroundings.

The types of entrepreneurs vary depending on background, country, and even sector, but the five most common types are:

1. Innovators
2. Hustlers
3. Imitators
4. Researchers
5. Buyers

Each of these different types of entrepreneurs has its own rules for business success. Still, most entrepreneurs go through similar struggles in finance, marketing, people, and even managing themselves.

Let's take a look at some different types of entrepreneurs, their roles, and how each type affects the success of the business:

1. Innovators

Innovators are entrepreneurs who come up with entirely new ideas and turn them into viable businesses.

These entrepreneurs usually change how people think about and do things. Such entrepreneurs tend to be highly passionate and obsessive, deriving their motivation from the unique nature of their business idea.

To say that innovators like Steve Jobs, Larry Page of Google, and Microsoft founder Bill Gates were obsessed with their businesses would be an understatement.

Advantages of Being An Innovate Entrepreneur:

1. Take all of the credit for the company's success (and all of the arrows).
2. Create the rules.
3. Face minimal competition during the initial days.

Disadvantages of Being An Innovate Entrepreneur:

1. You will need a lot of capital to bring a new idea to life.
2. They often face resistance from shareholders.
3. The timeframe for success is longer.
4. The ability of an innovative entrepreneur to envision a new way of thinking makes them stand out from the crowd and wildly successful in many cases. However, it takes significant capital, patience, and commitment to bring true innovation to life.

2. The Entrepreneurial Hustler

Unlike innovators, whose vision is the gas in their engine, hustlers work harder and are willing to get their hands dirty. Hustlers often start small and think about effort instead of raising capital to grow their businesses. These entrepreneurs focus on creating small to become more significant in the future.

Hustlers are motivated by their dreams and will work extremely hard to achieve them. They tend to be very focused and eliminate all forms of distraction, favoring risks over short-term comfort.

A perfect example of a hustler is Mark Cuban. He started in business very young, selling trash bags, newspapers, and even postage stamps, and later created a goldmine that internet giant Yahoo acquired!

Advantages of Being A Hustler

1. They will outwork most
2. Tend to have thick skin—they don't give up easily.
3. See disappointment and rejection as just a step in the process.

Disadvantages of Being A Hustler

1. Usually prone to burnout.
2. Wear out team members who don't have the same work ethic.
3. They often don't see the value of raising capital instead of just working harder.
4. Even though many hustlers never give up, many are willing to try anything to succeed, which unfortunately means they have many hits and misses. Achieving their

dreams takes a lot longer than most other types of entrepreneurs.

3. Imitators

These are the types of entrepreneurs who copy specific business ideas and improve upon them. They are always looking for ways to improve a particular product to gain the upper hand in the market.

Imitators are part innovators and part hustlers who don't stick to the terms set by others and have a lot of self-confidence.

The Advantages of Imitators

1. Refining a business idea is more accessible and less stressful.
2. You can easily benchmark your performance with the original idea.
3. Can learn and avoid mistakes that the originator made.

Disadvantages of Imitators

1. Their ideas are often compared to the original idea.
2. You always have to play catch-up.
3. Taking an existing idea and refining and improving it can be a great way to develop a business. It certainly does not have as much risk as the innovator, but it might not be as sexy.

4. Researcher

Even after having an idea, researchers will take their time to gather all the relevant information about it. To them, failure is not an option because they have analyzed the picture from all angles.

Researchers believe in starting a business that has a high chance of succeeding because they have put in detailed work to understand all aspects. As a result, these entrepreneurs usually take a lot of time to launch products and make decisions because they need a foundation of deep understanding. These entrepreneurs rely much more on data and facts than on instincts and intuition. For a researcher, there should be no room for making mistakes.

The Advantages of Being a Research Entrepreneur

1. Plan for as many contingencies as possible.
2. Write detailed, well-thought-out business and financial plans.
3. Focus on data and information rather than gut feelings.
4. They won't start unless they feel like they know the market.
5. Will minimize the chances of failing in the business

Disadvantages of Being an Entrepreneurial Researcher

1. It usually moves slowly.
2. Doesn't like risk, which can hamper progress in a new venture.
3. Even though these types of entrepreneurs spend a lot of time researching and digging into the data to ensure

the success of their business, they can fall into the habit of obsessing over the numbers and focusing less on the company's running.

5. Buyers

One thing that defines buyers is their wealth. These types of entrepreneurs have the money and specialize in buying profitable businesses.

Buyer entrepreneurs will identify a business and assess its viability, proceed to acquire it, and find the most suitable person to run and grow it.

Advantages of Being a Buyer

1. Buying an already established venture is less risky.
2. Doesn't have to worry so much about innovation.
3. Can focus on building on something that has already gone through building a foundation and already has a market for your products.

Disadvantages of Being a Buyer

1. Usually, they pay a high price for good business.
2. You will face the risk of buying businesses that have problems that you think you can turn around.

Chapter 4

AN ENTREPRENEUR WORKING 9-5

A 9–5 is a godsend for an entrepreneur.

Working in a 9–5 job, Monday–Friday, "for the man" is precisely the step to take if you are intent on becoming an entrepreneur. It's perfect. Honestly, perfect. Nobody wants to hear that, but it is.

There's no denying that working a 9-5 is difficult. A 9 to 5 gives you everything you need and more. It gives you structure, pace, colleagues, management, rules, and discipline. All the things you need if you're going to survive on your own. But most people don't see it that way. Most people get the 9–5 all wrong.

Often, the 9–5 is a destination. An unfair, unappealing one. One that is full of rules, regulations, bad bosses, and insufferable office politics. The headlines pour in, trivializing office life and simplifying the complicated. Just quit, they tell us. Life is too short to be cooped up in a square box.

People dig into the cheap suits, the bad coffee, and the painful small talk. They get fixated on the "I hate my job" culture too hard.

They spend all their time thinking about all the things they'd rather be doing with their time rather than the perfect situation that they've got right in front of them. Job haters spend their time thinking about the following:

- How to escape the 9–5 hole: what else could they be doing instead?
- Search the internet for other people and what they are doing.
- They dream about the life they could have had if they had made different decisions.
- Fixated how much they hate their boss, coworkers, and company.

But a 9–5 job provides a brilliant opportunity to dream big and work hard. You're just looking at it all wrong. A 9—5 teaches you an incredible amount. A 9–5 is the perfect test bed for any budding entrepreneur to find their feet and voice before going out alone. You're just looking at it all wrong. Working a 9 to 5 teaches discipline, structure, routine, and work ethic. Great managers teach you how to motivate a team, create a culture, and resolve conflicts; bad managers teach you the same lessons. There's more, though. The 9–5 gives you a taste of corporate life. It gives you a flavor of what happens if you stick around in a place for a while. It gives you a taste of where you don't want to be and encourages you not to get stuck.

Not enough? Well, here are some more things that a 9–5 teaches you:

* * *

How to manage your own time to meet your deadlines. How to deal with conflict.

How to manage stress.
How to present and capture an audience.
But more

Working 9–5 gives you the time to think about what you want to do with your life. Whether you have a bee in your bonnet about being an entrepreneur or are dead set on a career move, a 9–5 gives you the space to think. It gives you time to reflect on what you want to do with your life to optimize for happiness. And that's something. Perhaps most importantly, it allows you to explore your creative pursuits without much risk. Working a 9 to 5 pays the bills while you explore what you want to do outside of it. If you decide tomorrow that you want to start a training company, but six months later, it goes downhill, you than that, a 9 to 5 gives you time.

Won't lose your house as a result. You won't lose much because you have the security of your 9-5 job. You '9–5 act as a buffer. If you keep your 9–5 job, you can explore endless side hustles until you find the one for you. That could take months, or it could take years. It doesn't matter.

Quitting isn't the answer; it's a step.

The number of stories I've read about a budding entrepreneurs starting a side hustle and, after a week, quitting their job to pursue it is admirable. But what is not spoken of is the stress, anxiety, and sleepless nights after said side hustle goes down the pan. Here's the typical story:

The 9–5 worker hates his job. He complains and decides that he will start a business, follow his dreams and quit the 'rat race. He leaves, and he's off. He's flying. High on his supply of giving the middle finger to the corporate world, he's high. Then, after a few weeks, he realizes that the sales aren't coming in. He's quit in haste, and now he's a little stuck. All his time is spent applying for new jobs instead of following his dreams. He's back at a 9-5 with lower pay after a year.

Quitting is easy. Sustaining the aftermath isn't. Stories that start as a motivation to 'quit your job today' often end in tears later down the line because the stories miss one crucial point.

DATA

You need to gather data to prove that your actions are feasible. Whether people have a desire for your product and whether that is viable, i.e., you can make money from it. All of this takes time, and to sustain yourself for a long time, you need money. And you can collect that data while still working 9-5.

Takeaway

We get the 9–5 wrong. The 9–5 is an excellent test bed for you and your future endeavors. A 9-5 is brilliant whether you want to start a business, build an empire, or create a company of one. Alongside the many lessons it will teach you, it will give you the space and time to think about what you want to do. After that, it will provide you with the finances to test concepts, plan out businesses and launch ideas without the worry that if it all goes wrong, you're back to square one.

A 9–5 is the perfect business plan for an entrepreneur. Willingness to take chances Business owners who are willing to take chances tend to achieve more than those who play it safe.

START YOUR BUSINESS AROUND YOUR 9-TO-5 JOB

Some of you have asked, 'How do I balance becoming an entrepreneur while still keeping up my 9-to-5 job?' For the answer, I go back to a fundamental question: What are you trying to achieve with your life?

Do you want to live your dream lifestyle before your life ends? If the answer is yes, you have to begin to change the way you use your time so you can focus on creating the business.

We are going to assume you cannot leave your job. You have dependents or other responsibilities relying on you to provide a steady income. However, if you were an entrepreneur running your own business, you could earn a more consistent income.

So you go into this process with the desire to start your own business. You want to be an entrepreneur, and you know you will have to make changes to accomplish your goals.

Next, recognize how much time you have available to work on your business. You say your job is 9-to-5 – which means you are working just over 2,000 hours a year (probably less).

That's right, and you have more than three times as many hours to work on your business compared to your time at your job. So what was that you were saying about working around your day job?

The question you should be asking is: how do I convert the time I'm using for other activities to working on my business?

1. Determine what you want to do with the extra time.

> First, deciding what you want to do with your time is critical. If you start looking for time before deciding what to do with it, you could end up wasting the minutes you have available. You need to identify the activities you will be doing to start your business. Imagine you are not going to your job and have all the time in the world daily to work on your business. Where would you start?

If you do not have a business idea, spend the time researching possible products or services you could provide to the marketplace.

If you have a business idea, spend the time researching how you will turn your idea into a business, and map out every activity you need to do to get the business open.

If you already have a struggling business, spend the time re-assessing how to take advantage of the assets you have already built and researching options for growing your business.

Once you have decided what you want to do with your time, you will begin trading off activities that do not add value to your life for those that will get you to your dream lifestyle.

2. Start looking for time/activity trade-offs

You have to decide what is more important to you.

To start your business, you need time to work on your business and to find the time you have to trade off from other activities you do. If you are serious about reaching lifestyle freedom, you have to be prepared to make these changes in your life now. If you have dependents who will not relieve you from your financial responsibilities, that is, if you keep your day job to pay the bills, they should give you back some time.

Remember, you are working on getting to lifestyle freedom. Once you've achieved it, you will have all the time in the world to do everything you want to do.

To trade off your time, you should be honest and prepared. If you are in a family where the term "family is everything" means giving up on yourself for appearances' sake, you should have a serious discussion with your dependents.

Begin by envisioning your dream lifestyle together. Maybe family members feel like you do. The work grind and answering to others is not the world you want to stay in forever. Get your family to see the value of taking time now to step away from all the false obligations of attending every event – and focus on moving you forward in your dreams. You can do this precisely because 'family is everything.' You want more time with them, more freedom to do what you want, and more stability and security in your professional life.

Making a change can be a challenging step because we are programmed to believe that we must be 'social.' But outside of once-in-a-lifetime activities like weddings (okay, some will be twice), where you wish to share the joy of someone you care about, and funerals, where you wish to pay your last respects, there are few events that you absolutely must attend. Of course, people will have special birthdays or graduations, but often the event is another party with the same set of people engaged in conversations, drinking, and eating.

You must make a stand for your life vision and turn them down.

When you pitch to your dependents that you need time, you should begin with your plan to achieve lifestyle freedom. Short-term pain for long-term gain. The conversation does not start with, "I'm not going to Aunt Martha's birthday party because I might want to look at some stuff about starting a business." You can replace some dependent or friend-related time-wasting activities with more efficient practices. Maybe you go to the mall every weekend because that's when you spend time together. But you can do all your shopping online and have products delivered. Use the time you would usually be driving to the mall, looking for parking, and fighting crowds to spend time together. And use the time you would generally wander around the mall to work on your business.

Engage your dependents in business planning. Kids love to surf the Internet. Let them be involved in doing research, especially to look at your potential market and the competitive environment.

4. Use the time to create your business.

You will be thanking yourself as you push closer to your dream lifestyle. Take all the time you have found or created with more efficient practices and focus on getting where you want to go.

You know you are going to make changes to achieve your dream lifestyle. So make changes now on the road to getting there. You'll be happy that you did. Here's the math: You have 24 hours a day for 365 or 366 days. That equals 8,760 or 8,784. You work 9-to-5. That's 8 hours a day, five days a week, 52 weeks of the year, or 2,080 hours. That assumes you never take a holiday or a personal day. There are ten statutory federal holidays, and most people get at least ten personal days.

So that's another 160 hours you are not working and bringing your total to under 2,000.

HOW TO START A BUSINESS WHILE WORKING

Starting a business while employed can be a great way to test your business idea— here's how to make it work.

For many people, quitting a salaried job to start a business is an unaffordable luxury. With bills to pay and families to support, many have no option but to keep the day job while building their new company—necessitating a delicate juggling act fraught with stress, complexity, and potential conflicts of interest. However, There's no reason why you can't serve two masters at once.

Some of the world's top companies have begun as side projects, fostered in the founder's bedroom during evenings and weekends. Balancing a salaried role with a start-up can have advantages, enabling you to gain contacts and advice while testing your commitment to the company you wish to found.

Living a two-job existence will never be an easy task, but here are some ways to get it done:

1. CREATE A CLEAR SCHEDULE.

At the outset, you must create a clear, realistic timeline for starting your business, breaking down the process into achievable goals. That way, you will always be clear about exactly where you're up to—vital in maintaining focus and avoiding frustration.

Priorities are the most important tasks which will take the longest time, such as securing insurance, completing the necessary registration, and applying for start-up funding. If you leave these until the end, you could face exasperating last-minute delays.

2. THINK ABOUT APPROACHING YOUR BOSS.

Wendy Tan White founded Moon fruit's web development company while working at internet bank Egg. She told us: "Don't think you can't go and speak to your boss. Even if you haven't got that close a relationship, most companies want to keep their staff, and even if they can only keep your part-time, it might be worthwhile.

Many employers are entrepreneurs themselves and will appreciate the fact that you've shown initiative – exceptionally if you choose your words Carefully.

Christian Lang, who started the Trade shift while working for the Danish government, told us: "You should demonstrate to your bosses that what you're doing is a compliment to them. Tell them why it will help the existing workplace, flatter their ego, and give them credit."

3. Use your holidays.

If you want to get your business up and running quickly, you'll need to use all the time available – and annual leave provides a critical window of opportunity. Furthermore, by using your holidays for work rather than pleasure, you could make financial savings towards your start-up.

Your family may not appreciate that you're devoting holidays to work, but hopefully, when your company takes off, they'll see the benefits of the decision.

4. Get into a routine

As anyone who has ever reviewed for an exam knows, the structure is crucial to working effectively at home. It is doubly important if you've already worked a full day, so you need to plan out a routine for your start-up, identifying the exact time you'll be starting work each evening and the time you'll be logging off for the night. Once you've created your schedule, make sure you stick to it. Don't take refuge in excuses that allow you to procrastinate, and don't work a minute beyond your finish time. The more disciplined you can be, the better. Maximize the resources available.

Tristram Mayhew, who founded Go Ape! while holding a senior position at General Electric, said:

"I spent many late nights thinking it through, writing and making plans on the internet. A lot of the market research was available on the internet – it's extraordinary how much you can get. " I also talked it through with friends with relevant backgrounds, particularly accountancy backgrounds, in the evenings. People will be generous with their time, so you should ask for as much advice as possible. With things like cash-flow forecasting, everyone needs as much help as they can get.

5. Get support

You may have always dreamed of standing entirely on your own two feet. However, if you want to build a successful start-up without quitting your current job, you may need someone else's support.

6. Choose a good location.

When you're juggling two jobs, every minute counts — you have to make the very best of all the time you have available. So you must find a location that works for you and allows you to achieve maximum productivity without distraction.

7. Avoid cross-over

In the age of smartphones, tablets, and personal email addresses, there's no reason to bring your start-up activity into your day job — the two can be kept entirely separate.

Be fair and careful about how you use email, IT, and things like that— companies usually have rules about how you use their equipment. Use Hotmail or Yahoo! mail to generate correspondence about your start-up; don't use your work account.

So that there's no conflict or interruption, I would advise setting up Another phone number so that you don't have people calling you at the office regarding your new business venture. 8. Behave with respect.

Ultimately, as each of the entrepreneurs we spoke with stressed, you must behave respectfully. Your current employer could be a potential customer, supplier, or investor one day, so try not to burn your bridges. You might hate your salaried job, but it's still important to be professional – what goes around comes around, and if you mistreat your boss, they'll remember it.

Are you starting a new small business? Find out where to begin and how to achieve success.

You want to ensure you prepare thoroughly before starting a business, but realize that things will almost certainly go awry. To run a successful business, you must adapt to changing situations.

Conducting in-depth market research on your field and the demographics of your potential clientele is an essential part of crafting a business plan. Researching involves running surveys, holding focus groups, and researching SEO and public data. Before you start selling your product or service, you need to build up your brand and get a following of people ready to jump on board when you open your doors for business.

Chapter 5

SEVEN COMPELLING REASONS TO START A BUSINESS.

Building a successful company requires more than just a brilliant idea. To start a company, you should have stamina and be passionate about your business concept. But it may be worthwhile. A little decision-making assistance for anyone considering going self-employed

SEVEN REASONS FOR ESTABLISHING:

1. THE ACT OF FOUNDING CONFERS LIBERTY AND INDEPENDENCE.

Entrepreneurs make their own decisions and operate on their own. There is no time clock or boss to tell you when you can go on vacation. Entrepreneurs work for themselves.

2. FOUNDERS WORK WITH ZEAL.

When you work for yourself, you work more passionately. It takes a lot of energy, time, and effort to start your own business. Those who work with dedication and passion, on the other hand, know why they get up in the morning.

3. ANYONE WHO WANTS TO START A BUSINESS WILL FIND PLENTY OF HELP.

If you want to start a business, you will receive a lot of help and advice. There are state assistance programs and advisory services for start-up competitions and initiatives. A mentor can also provide assistance and advice before and during the start-up phase. If you have a good business idea, you can raise funds by crowdfunding and even build a small fan base simultaneously.

5. ENTREPRENEURS CONTINUE TO LEARN THROUGHOUT THEIR LIVES.

Founders are frequently lone wolves or work in small teams, at least in the early stages. They often take on tasks for which large corporations have specialists. Customer acquisition, accounting, and employee motivation are all areas where entrepreneurs must learn new skills and educate themselves. To put it another way, they're constantly learning new skills they didn't know they had.

5. SOMETIMES, A LAPTOP IS ALL YOU NEED FOR YOUR OWN BUSINESS.

In recent years, digitization and networking have made it easier to establish and organize a business. IT start-ups, in particular, can get by with few resources at first. Having your laptop in the living room is frequently sufficient. Small-scale online shopping via Internet platforms like Dawanda or eBay can easily be arranged.

6. A PROFITABLE BUSINESS CAN BE A GOOD RETIREMENT PLAN.

If you want to maintain your standard of living, you must plan for retirement. A well-managed business can be an excellent way to prepare for life after work.

7. A FOUNDATION IS NOT A PERMANENT DECISION.

Finally, starting a business does not bind you to it for the rest of your life. Life can change, and you may prefer to return to work later. A company can be sold again in the future.

HOW TO START A SMALL BUSINESS

1. Refine your idea.
2. Write a business plan.
3. Assess your finances.
4. Determine your legal business structure.
5. Register with the government and IRS
6. Purchase an insurance policy.

7. Build your team!

8. Choose your vendors.

9. Brand yourself and advertise.

10. Grow your business.

1. Refine your idea.

> If you're considering starting a business, you likely already know what you want to sell online or the market you wish to enter. Do a quick search for existing companies in your chosen industry. Learn what current brand leaders are doing and figure out how you can do it better. If you think your business can deliver something that other companies don't (or give the same thing, only faster and cheaper), or if you've got a solid idea and are ready to create a business plan,

> Define your "why." In the words of Simon Sinek, 'always start with why,' "Glenn Gutek, CEO of Awake Consulting and Coaching, told Business News Daily. "It is good to know why you are launching your business. In this process, it may be wise to differentiate between whether the company serves a personal why or a marketplace why. When your business is concentrated on meeting a need in the market, the scope of your business will always be more significant than a business designed to serve a personal call."

> Consider franchising.

> Another option is to open a franchise of an established company. The concept, brand following, and business model are already

in place; you need a good location and the means to fund your operation.

Brainstorm your business name.

Regardless of which option you choose, it's vital to understand the reasoning behind your idea. Stephanie Desaulniers, owner of Business by Dezign and former director of operations and women's business programs at Convention Center, cautions entrepreneurs against writing a business plan or brainstorming a business name before nailing down the idea's value.

TIP: To refine your business idea, identify your "why," your target customers, and your business name.

2. Write a business plan.

Once you have your idea in place, you need to ask yourself a few critical questions: What is the purpose of your business? Who are your customers? What are your end goals? How will you finance your startup costs? Inquiries can be answered in a well-written business plan.

A lot of mistakes are made by new businesses rushing into things without pondering these aspects of the company. You need to find your target customer base. Who is going to buy your product or service? If you can't find evidence that there's a demand for your idea, then what would be the point?

Perform market research.

Conducting thorough market research on your field and the demographics of potential clients is an integral part of crafting a business plan.

You are conducting surveys, holding focus groups, and researching SEO and public data. The best small businesses have differentiated products or services from the competition. Standing out significantly impacts your competitive landscape and allows you to convey unique value to potential customers.

Consider an exit strategy.

It's also a good idea to consider an exit strategy as you compile your business plan. You are having a plan for how you'll exit the business forces you to think about the future.

According to Josh Tolley, CEO of both Shyft Capital and Kavana, "too often, new entrepreneurs are so excited about their business and so certain that everyone everywhere will be a customer that they give very little, if any, time to show the plan on leaving the business."

When you board an airplane, what is the first thing they show you? How to get off of it. When you go to a movie, what do they point out before the feature begins to play? Where the exits are In your first week of kindergarten, they line up all the kids and teach them fire drills to exit the building. Too many times, I have witnessed business leaders that don't have three or four predetermined exit routes. Poor exit strategy has led to lower company value and destroyed family relationships.

A business plan helps you figure out where your company is going, how it will overcome potential difficulties, and what you need to sustain it. When you're ready to put pen to paper, these free templates can help.

3. Assess your finances.

Starting any business has a price, so you must determine how to cover those costs. Do you have the means to fund your startup, or will you need to borrow money? If you're planning to leave your current job to focus on your business, do you have money to support yourself until you profit?

It's best to find out how much your startup costs will be.

Many startups fail because they run out of money before turning a profit. It's never a bad idea to overestimate the amount of startup capital you need, as it can be a while before the business begins to bring in sustainable revenue.

Perform a break-even analysis.

One way you can determine how much money you need is to perform a break-even analysis. Investigation is an essential element of financial planning that helps business owners determine when their company, product, or service will be profitable.

The formula is simple:

Fixed Costs Ã· (Average Price – Variable Costs) = Break-Even Point

Every entrepreneur should use this formula as a tool because it informs you about the minimum performance your business must achieve to avoid losing money. Furthermore, it helps you understand exactly where your profits come from, so you can set production goals accordingly.

Here are the three most common reasons for conducting a break-even analysis:

1. Determine profitability. It is generally every business owner's highest interest.

2. Ask yourself: How much revenue do I need to generate to cover all my expenses? Which products or services turn a profit, and which ones sell at a loss?

3. Set a price for a product or service. When most people think about pricing, they consider how much their product costs to create and how competitors are pricing their products.

4. Ask yourself: What are the fixed rates, what are the variable costs, and what is the total cost? What is the price of any physical goods? What is the price of labor?

5. Examine the data. What volume of goods or services do you have to sell to be profitable?

6. Ask yourself: How can I reduce my overall fixed costs? How can I reduce the variable price per unit? How can I improve sales?

Watch your expenses.

Don't overspend when starting a business. Understand the purchases that make sense for your business and avoid overspending on fancy new equipment that won't help you achieve your business goals.

4. Determine your legal business structure.

   Before registering your company, you must decide what entity it is. Your business structure legally affects everything from how you file your taxes to your liability if something goes wrong.

   Ultimately, it is up to you to determine which type of entity is best for your current needs and future business goals. It's essential to learn about the various legal business structures available. If you're struggling to make up your mind, it's not a bad idea to discuss the decision with a business or legal advisor.

5. Register with the government and the Internal Revenue Service.

   You must acquire various business licenses before you can legally operate your business. For example, you must register your business with federal, state, and local governments. There are several documents you must repair before registering. Articles of incorporation and operating agreements

   To become an officially recognized business entity, you must register with the government. Corporations need an "articles of incorporationâ€ document, which includes your business name, business purpose, corporate structure, stock details, and other information about your company. Similarly, some LLCs will need to Create an operating agreement.

DBA (doing business as)

If you don't have articles of incorporation or an operating agreement, you will need to register your business name, which can be your legal name, a fictitious DBA name (if you are the sole proprietor), or the name you've come up with for your company. You may also want to take steps to trademark your business name for extra legal protection.

Most states require you to get a DBA. If you're in a general partnership or a proprietorship operating under a fictitious name, you may need to apply for a DBA certificate. It's best to contact or visit your local county clerk's office and ask about specific requirements and fees. Generally, there is a registration fee involved.

6. Purchase an insurance policy.

It might slip your mind as something you'll "get around to" eventually, but purchasing the right insurance for your business is a crucial step before you officially launch. Dealing with incidents such as property damage, theft, or even a customer lawsuit can be costly, and you need to be sure that you're adequately protected.

Although you should consider several types of business insurance, there are a few basic insurance plans that can benefit small businesses. For example, if your business will have employees, you will at least need to purchase workers' compensation and unemployment insurance.

You may also need other types of coverage, depending on your location and industry. Still, most small businesses are required to purchase general liability (GL) insurance or a business owner's policy. GL covers property damage, bodily injury, and personal injury to you or a third party. If your business provides a service, you You may also want to consider professional liability insurance. It covers if you do something wrong or neglect to do something you should have done while operating your business.

7. Build your team.

Unless you're planning to be your only employee, you must recruit and hire a great team to get your company off the ground. Joe Zawadzki, CEO and founder of MediaMath, said entrepreneurs need to give the "people" element of their businesses the same attention they give their products.

Understanding what gaps exist and determining how and when you will address them should be a top priority. Figuring out how the team will work together is equally important. Defining roles and responsibilities, division of labor, how to give feedback, or how to work together when not everyone is in the same room will save you a lot of headaches down the line."

8. Choose your vendors.

Running a business can be overwhelming, and you and your team probably aren't able to do it all on your own. That's where third-party vendors come in. Companies in every industry, from HR to business phone systems, exist to partner with you and help you run your business better.

When searching for B2B partners, you'll have to choose carefully. These companies will have access to vital and potentially sensitive business data, so it's critical to find someone you can trust. In our guide to choosing business partners, our expert sources recommended asking potential vendors about their experience in your industry, their track record with existing clients, and what kind of growth they've helped other clients achieve.

Not every business will need the same types of vendors, but there are everyday products and services that almost every industry will need. Consider the following functions that are a necessity for any business:

Taking payments from customers: Offering multiple payment options will ensure you can make a sale in whatever format is most accessible for your target customer.

9. Brand yourself and advertise.

- Before you start selling your product or service, you need to build up your brand and get a following of people ready to jump on board when you open your literal or figurative doors for business.

- Company website. Take your reputation online and build a company website. Many customers turn to the internet to learn about a business, and a website is a digital proof that your small business exists. It is also a great way to interact with current and potential customers.
- Social media. Use social media to spread the word about your new business, perhaps as a promotional tool to offer coupons and discounts to followers once you launch. The best social media platforms to utilize will depend on your target audience.
- CMR. The best CMR software solutions allow you to store customer data to improve how you market to them. A well-thought-out email marketing campaign can do wonders for reaching customers and communicating with your audience. To be successful, you will want to build your email marketing contact list strategically.
- Logo. Please create a logo to help people easily identify your brand and consistently use it across your platforms.

"These forms usually pertain to email communication and are often used in e-commerce to request permission to send newsletters, marketing material, product sales, etc., to customers," Edmonson said. "People get so many throwaway emails and other messages these days that, by getting them to opt into your services transparently, you begin to build trust with your customers."

10. Grow your business.

> Your launch and first sales are only the beginning of your task as an entrepreneur. To make a profit and stay afloat, you always need to grow your business. It's going to take time and effort, but you'll get out of your business what you put into it. Collaborating with more established brands in your industry is a great way to achieve growth. Reach out to other companies and ask for some promotion in exchange for a free product sample or service. Partner with a charity organization, and volunteer some of your time or products to get your name out there.
>
> While these tips will help launch your business and get you set to grow, there's never a perfect plan. You want to ensure you prepare thoroughly for starting a business, but things will almost certainly go awry. To run a successful business, you must adapt to changing situations.

HOW TO START A BUSINESS FROM SCRATCH WITH (ALMOST) NO MONEY

Creating a business plan and starting a business can seem daunting and complicated. There are numerous factors to consider, ranging from coming up with a great idea to registering a company to business planning, fundraising, and more:

That's why we've put together this comprehensive guide to take you step-by-step through starting a business. It covers everything you could

Want to know about starting a business, including:

- Before you start, get to know yourself as an entrepreneur.
- Find out why you want to start a business.
- Examination of the feasibility of your ideas
- Real-world testing of your business premises
- Creation of a preliminary business plan
- Creation of the correct legal form for your company
- Understanding of your financial, accounting, and tax obligations
- Protecting your business from legal and natural disasters (insurance)
- Creating an identity for your business, including developing a brand and website,
- Set up your business needs like internet and stationery.
- Creation of the first marketing and sales strategies
- Assemble your first team, including recruitment, management, and company culture.
- Starting a business and working full-time at the same time

1. BEFORE YOU START, GET TO KNOW YOURSELF AS AN ENTREPRENEUR.

Starting a business is a lengthy process requiring much thought and consideration. First, you need to assess your strengths, weaknesses, and abilities. Assessment allows you to think about what you can and cannot do. Even if you have the world's most outstanding business idea, this is where you should start, as you may not have the skills or personality traits to turn it into a successful business. You want to think of business ideas that naturally fit your success, such as:

- A person with good programming skills is well suited to starting a web development agency.
- Accounting-related business may not be suitable for someone with a short attention span.
- A person who doesn't like meeting new people wouldn't be interested in working for a customer-centric company.

These are just three general examples, but they illustrate the thought process. The key is understanding yourself and your team and whether you are a good fit for a particular business idea, line of business, or type of business. It lets you start brainstorming ideas and narrowing down the kinds of companies you could create.

2. FIND OUT WHY YOU WANT TO START A BUSINESS.

Before starting a business, you should be sure of your motivation. There are numerous reasons that someone would trade the security of a job and career for the uncertainty of starting a business. So, the more specific you are about what you want to achieve, the better your chances of success.

Wealth, power, fame, or saving the world? Most entrepreneurs are motivated by a combination of the above, even if they don't want to admit it. Understanding what motivates you to start a business is a crucial factor in deciding what type of business to start. Why? Because it's far more likely to fail if a company you create does not match your ambitions.

Right from the start, you should make sure that your personal goals and your drive are compatible with your company. For example,

Someone looking for wealth might want to consider companies in the financial services industry, where fintech valuations and earnings are typically much higher than other startups.

Someone seeking power and influence could do so through any media Business.

Someone who aspires to fame may be best suited for a career in the entertainment industry.

To save the world, you might start a company that fights climate change with renewable energy.

It's essential to understand why you're starting a business so you can focus on business ideas that will get you where you want to be.

3. MAKE SURE THERE'S A GOOD REASON FOR IT

In reality, you probably don't just have one reason to start a business; instead, it is perhaps a combination of several. Note that the goals may conflict with each other. For example, creating a long-term family business that passes through the generations may not be compatible with acquiring a sizeable fortune. You may find that you need to sell the business to realize its total value.

While it's possible to start a successful business to make a lot of money, it becomes difficult if there isn't at least one other motivator. It can take many years before you start a business and get any money-if ever-and; the amount of hard work required along the way is enormous, and the risk of failure is genuine.

Pinning your hopes on a potential pot of gold in the future is unlikely enough to get you through the trying times. So make sure you have a good reason, work hard, and have fun!

4. RECOGNIZE YOUR ENTREPRENEURIAL INTERESTS

When starting a business, having a passion for it increases your chances of success. The main reason for this is simple: you will work harder and more persistently on a business you are passionate about and increase your chances of Success. Passion is often the only difference between an entrepreneur who starts a successful business and one that fails.

Logic dictates that if you want to start a successful business, you should begin in an area you are passionate about. To determine what companies or places of business you are or could be passionate about, consider the areas, activities, etc., that interest you and have strong opinions about, such as: e.g.,

- Someone who enjoys hiking should consider starting a travel company. Someone who appreciates Lego might consider beginning a toy or construction company.

- Someone who has lived their whole life with a passion for music can start a sound-related business.

When considering offline or online business ideas, remember that starting a business is difficult enough. However, if you choose one that you are passionate about, you will be far more likely to be successful.

DEVELOPMENT OF EXCELLENT BUSINESS CONCEPTS

Developing a business idea is easy; it's challenging to come up with a great business idea. When starting, you must explore as many ideas as possible before deciding which ones to pursue.

In this section, we'll walk you through turning a great business idea into a successful, profitable, and valuable venture.

◆ START CREATING BUSINESS CONCEPTS.

It is the time to generate ideas. It can be a long and time-consuming process, but with a bit of patience, you'll be able to bring some fantastic ones to life. Below are tips on how to start the ideation process and generate great business ideas.

◆ SOLVE A PROBLEM THAT INTERESTS POTENTIAL CUSTOMERS

Start by thinking about what fundamental problems you could solve and how. Many successful companies started with the goal of solving real issues affecting millions of people and offering a solution through their products and services.

For example, Tesla started with the goal of making all the cars in the world electric, and they're well on their way, having built a hugely successful multibillion-dollar business in the process.

◆ DETERMINE WHERE YOU CAN OFFER A BETTER SOLUTION.

Look for areas where solutions are already available but where you can outperform existing companies in terms of efficiency, innovation, or cost.

For example, Apple entered the mobile phone market as an underdog with a new innovative product more than a decade ago and is now the market leader. Even though the technology had been available for years, nobody had brought to market the level of innovation that the iPhone had.

◆ BE CHEAPER THAN THE COMPETITION.

Look for areas where you can offer your customers significant savings over competitors. This type of company grows extremely fast, especially during recessions.

Pound land, for example, is an excellent example of this type of business; since its inception, it has used price as its primary differentiator from its competitors. By offering the lowest possible prices on a wide range of consumer goods, the company has grown into a highly successful retail chain.

◆ INNOVATE IN A TRADITIONAL, SLOWLY CHANGING MARKET

Is there any company or industry where this is often the case in non-tech sectors that have been slow to embrace change while maintaining unprofitable status?

These industries often have enormous opportunities to be disrupted by new technologies, innovations, systems, and methods. For example, the taxi industry recently changed dramatically with the introduction of Uber, which has revolutionized how we find and hire taxis.

◆ CREATE A COMPANY TO FILL A FUTURE NEED OR MARKET

Think about the future: what will the world look like in 5 or 10 years? When you think about the future, you can consider new markets and niches that innovation and new technologies may create.

◆ BE BETTER BY EMULATING OTHER COMPANIES.

If you're not at the cutting edge of technology, your business ideas won't be unique. Many of the world's largest companies were not revolutionary, but they entered the markets with established players and outperformed everyone else.

You don't have the most innovative idea to start a successful business; you have to do it better than everyone else! For example, in the early 1990s, Microsoft emerged out of nowhere and defeated every other competitor to become the dominant operating system vendor.

◆ TURN YOUR INTERESTS INTO A BUSINESS

A logical next step is to turn a hobby into a legitimate business. Why? A hobby is something you already know a lot about, obviously enjoy, and know where to start. For example, it makes sense to switch from collecting to selling models.

◆ EXAMINE YOUR BUSINESS CONCEPTS

This stage is all about researching your business idea as thoroughly as possible to determine if your opinion or theories have the potential to become a successful business. To evaluate and compare them, you must first understand the following points.

Chapter 6

DEFINE AND RESEARCH YOUR TARGET MARKET

Is a market for your company, product, or service, and is it big enough to support your goals? You should also consider the competitive landscape and be clear about your main competitors. Examine yours and their weaknesses and strengths, as well as market opportunities and threats. You want a clear picture of the overall market and how your business fits into it.

1. CHECK IF THERE IS A MARKET FOR YOUR PRODUCT OR SERVICE.

Is your product or service in high demand, or do you need to educate customers about the need?

2. RECOGNIZE YOUR POTENTIAL CUSTOMERS

If you're selling B2B, you should have a good idea of who your prospects are, including demographic information and business details.

3. HAVE A LOGICAL MARKETING AND SALES STRATEGY.
Understanding how to reach potential customers and grow your market share is critical to success. Understand what marketing and sales activities and channels you need to track.

4. MAKE SURE YOUR BUSINESS MODEL IS VIABLE.

Is your business model viable, given the current market and potential customers? Many start-ups fail because their business model doesn't work. Find funding for your business.

Is it expensive to start your own business, so determining if your business will be prosperous, as it depends on your financial resources.

5. EXAMINE YOUR BUSINESS PREMISES

After thoroughly researching some business ideas, it's time to test and validate quickly whether the premise of your proposed business works in the real world. Many entrepreneurs who skip this stage waste a lot of time chasing ventures that will never work. Now that we've established that it's a good idea to test your ideas and do some research, this section looks at the different go-to-market routes for testing other ideas.

6. BE PRECISE WHEN MEASURING POWER.

When testing a proposed company, you can evaluate each company's performance in several ways. Therefore, it is crucial to determine what you want to measure to determine success or failure. To help you get started, you should consider the following actions:

- How much money could you make/how many products could you sell?
- What kind of customer interest can you generate?
- How much press and attention can you get?

7. WRITE A BUSINESS PLAN

In the beginning, writing a business plan can be a new, complicated, and sometimes overwhelming task. However, there are some golden rules to keep in mind when writing that will make your life much easier!

8. KEEP YOUR LETTER SHORT

Strive to summarize your writing and keep it as short as possible, as this will add clarity to your plan. It helps you organize your thoughts, but more importantly, it makes it much easier for others to understand.

9. MAKE SURE EVERYTHING IS RELEVANT

It's too easy and tempting to include irrelevant information in your business plan. This extra information usually makes your communication less efficient and the idea more challenging to understand.

To get rid of irrelevant material, do a quick review after completing a section and remove anything that doesn't support or complement the main point you're trying to make in that section.

10. CHECK YOUR GRAMMAR AND SPELLING CAREFULLY.

If you think outsiders might read your business plan, ensure correct spelling and grammar. When a document contains spelling and grammatical errors, it loses credibility and meaning.

- Provide an introductory mission statement.
- Set specific goals and explain how you intend to get there.

It may seem simple, but many entrepreneurs are unsure how they will achieve their business goals. Make sure you think hard about it and find a way for your business to get from point A to point B.

11. USE A REALISTIC TIMELINE

Open a business

Your specific needs will determine the structure you choose for your business. This section will walk you through the different business structures, their pros and cons, and how to set them up.

DIFFERENT TYPES OF BUSINESS STRUCTURES

When setting up a company, you can choose from various legal forms, which we will discuss below.

ONE-MAN BUSINESS

A sole proprietorship is a business in which one person owns and runs the entire operation. It's the most basic business structure you can use. It is ideal for one-person companies such as independent accountants, web developers, and gardeners, among others.

As a sole proprietorship, the individual is entitled to any/all profits made by the business but is also liable for any debt or damage incurred. There are currently over 3 million registered sole proprietors in the UK, and the number is growing due to a large influx of skilled freelancers.

A COMPANY WITH LIMITED LIABILITY

A limited liability company is a legal structure that indicates that a company is distinct from its owners. Meaning that the owners are only liable for any business debt up to the amount of their investment, limiting any risk for business owners beyond their total investment.

CHOOSING THE RIGHT CORPORATE STRUCTURE

There is no easy answer to which structure is best for your business. It depends on the operation and needs of your business. For example, let's say you:

- If you intend to expand your small business beyond yourself (one person) and then sell it; a limited liability company is the most suitable structure.
- If you intend to only operate as a one-person business shortly, a sole proprietorship is probably the best structure.
- If you intend to start a business that will require a significant amount of management and capital and provide services, a limited liability partnership is the best option.

Setting up a structure for your business isn't something you do every day. Conduct additional research and determine which legal form is best for your business.

SET UP FINANCE, ACCOUNTING, AND TAXES

Once you have determined the legal structure of your business, you need to figure out some key financial and tax responsibilities.

◆ ESTABLISHMENT OF A COMMERCIAL BANK ACCOUNT

Before you can start generating income or making purchases, you must first open a commercial bank account to transfer funds (money) from your company to send, receive, and keep safe.

◆ CHOOSING A BANK FOR YOUR BUSINESS

There is no easy answer; instead, gather information about each bank and its offerings and compare them to see who is the best fit. It would help if you looked for information like this:

- What is their track record with small businesses?
- Is a selection of products and information specifically geared towards small businesses?
- What do other business customers say about the bank?
- Is the bank reputable, and has it recently engaged in illegal activities?

It would be best if you had a good idea of which bank is best for your business after gathering all this information that you can find online.

◆ PROTECT YOUR BUSINESS

After resolving any financial concerns, you must protect your business from the unexpected by addressing specific legal and insurance matters.

◆ FIND A LAWYER OR LAW FIRM

Most businesses do not need to hire a legal advisor, to begin with, unless they want advice on setting up a business or have specific legal issues. At some point in your company's life cycle, however, you will need legal support, whether drafting contracts or representing you in court. When hiring legal counsel, always agree in advance on an hourly rate and the time required for all work.

◆ CHOOSING THE BEST COMMERCIAL INSURANCE

As with purchasing any product or service, you should shop around and compare prices and terms. When it comes to insurance, you should read the fine print carefully and clarify the duration of your policy (to ensure the policy fully covers loss or damage).

◆ CREATE YOUR COMPANY'S BRAND AND IDENTITY

Now that you've properly secured your business, it's time to create a public profile. How to present your business to the world, including branding, creating a simple website, and setting up a business email address. Create a professional brand for your business. A professional brand is crucial for any business looking to differentiate in today's competitive environment. At least an essential website is a requirement for doing business in the 21st century, whether you are a retail store, a chemical company, or a modeling company. Customers expect you to have a website and be able to find it easily. Your site should contain: Add and display your company/business information such as address, phone number, name, and logo (if you have a limited company number, it is also a legal requirement to include it here).

DESCRIBE WHAT YOUR COMPANY IS/DOES.

Provide information about your products and services. Provide a business email or contact form where potential customers or external parties can quickly contact you. It is just the essential information you need to provide on your website. You can add a lot more. So, how does one go about creating a website? It's a tempting idea because, even if your business fails, you'll still have a job, and if it succeeds, the transition to becoming your boss will be much less risky. So many people now do business from home in their free time in the evenings, and at weekends that they have their name – the 5 to 9ers.

◆ IDEAL BUSINESSES TO START IN YOUR FREE TIME

A web-based business that doesn't require your constant physical presence to function and can outsource many of its activities. Brent and Marilena Shaw, husband, and wife, run their online luggage business, SwissLuggage.com, in their free time in addition to their full-time job. They outsource the packing and shipping of orders to a fulfillment company, which takes their inventory and stores it in their warehouse. During the day, their customer inquiries are dealt with by a call center. One that allows you to communicate with clients via email instead of over the phone, freeing you from the constraints of traditional office hours.

Start a business that competes with the company you work for and do not start a business that uses information or data provided by your employer, as you will quickly run into legal trouble.

◆ HIDE YOUR BUSINESS INTENTIONS

Downplay your business intentions in front of your boss. No one wants to think that their co-worker's attention and focus lies elsewhere, no matter how well you get along. Provide information only when necessary and never bring up your business project in conversation unless specifically asked to do so.

HOW TO BE A SUCCESSFUL BUSINESS OWNER

Most business owners will tell you that starting a business is one of the most challenging and rewarding ways to earn a living. Being a successful business owner requires a considerable amount of hard work and dedication but also generally relies on personal qualities and business practices that are common characteristics of successful entrepreneurs. These characteristics lie as much in a business's founding principles as in its day-to-day operations and dictate every decision the entrepreneur makes. By following these guidelines, you can increase your chances of founding a successful business or getting your existing business back on track.

1. Focus and mindset

   Start a business that you're passionate about and knowledgeable about.

   That knowledge can come from either prior work experience or a personal hobby that you're ready to turn into a career. Even if a business idea seems highly profitable in theory, don't start that business unless your heart is in it. While profit is crucial, it likely won't keep you coming in early every day and driving growth.

For example, imagine you have experience making coffee as a barista or waiter and want to turn your passion for good coffee into a small business. You would already know a good amount about the industry and be able to apply not only your knowledge but your passion to your work.

2. Start with a well-defined purpose.

While the financial benefits of business ownership can be great, most successful business owners don't start with money in mind. To get your business off the ground, you'll need a clear purpose. This purpose should be something more intangible than money, like giving back to your community by creating jobs, solving a problem that you see in your daily life, or pursuing a passion. It doesn't mean that you shouldn't also strive for profitability, just that your primary goal should be the accomplishment of a greater purpose.

3. Understand your customers.

Before you get started, take some time to do market research and get to know your customers and your industry. The U.S. Small Business Administration provides a great deal of information on which services and products are in demand. You will also want to think about who will be buying your product or using your service and learn the best way to appeal to this population.

4. Find a first step instead of a destination.

   Always start with a business model that can be up and running quickly on a low budget. Too many small businesses begin with grandiose goals that require a large amount of startup capital and investors. However, successful companies will have a model that can operate on a smaller scale. It proves to potential investors that your idea is a valid way of making money and increases your odds of ever getting investment money (if that's what you're looking for).

5. Create a support network.

   One of the essential parts of successful business ownership is getting over your ego and seeking help. Your most significant sources of advice are going to be business associates and other professionals that share your goals. Surround yourself with knowledgeable and successful people and feed off of their ideas and enthusiasm.

6. Find a mentor.

   A good mentor is someone who has already run or is running a successful business of their own. A good example would be a family member or friend that has been successful in business. This mentor can help you with anything from knowing how to manage your employees to properly filing your taxes. Because their knowledge comes from direct experience, they can help you more personally than any other source could.

7. Efficient Operations

   At first, focus only on your primary operations.

   That is, avoid getting caught up in every business opportunity that comes your way. It's better to be perfect at one thing than mediocre at five. It applies to making decisions to diversify your business by taking on additional projects for yourself outside of your primary business. Focusing on one thing will allow you to commit your resources and be more productive in that endeavor.

8. Focus on cash flow, not profit.

   While making a profit should be one of your goals, it should not be your main focus when starting. Cash flow is far more significant. Small businesses run out of money before they have even been around long enough to generate earnings and must close their doors. Pay careful attention to your overhead costs and sales during the first years, and let profit take a back seat.

9. Keep detailed records.

   To be successful, you'll have to make a habit of recording every expense and revenue that your company has, as well as every dollar that flows through it. By knowing where your money is coming in and where it's going, you're more capable of recognizing financial difficulties before they arise. In addition, doing this will give you a better idea of where exactly you can make cuts to expenses or increase revenues.

10. Limit your expenses as much as possible.

While this may seem obvious, think of areas where you could generate the same effect by spending less money. Consider using pre-owned equipment, finding cheaper forms of advertising (for example, fliers rather than newspaper ads), or negotiating better payment terms with suppliers or customers to save a few dollars here and there. Try to maintain low spending habits and only spend money when and where you have to.

Consider supply chain efficiency.

Your costs, and therefore your revenue depends on a successful supply chain organization. By fostering good relationships with your suppliers, organizing deliveries, and consistently providing customers with timely service, you can increase your profitability and reputation. Successful supply chain management can also help you eliminate any part of your business with wasted resources, like raw materials or labor.

Consider finding strategic partners.

A good mentor and a strategic partner can help grow your business. Foster strategic partnerships by reaching out to companies you think could benefit yours, whether they are suppliers, technology providers, or complementary businesses. A good relationship with another business can provide you both with free advertising, lower your costs of doing business, or allow you to expand to new markets, depending on the partners you choose.

Be responsible when it comes to debt.

It's important that you realistically assess your ability to pay back any debt that you take on. While starting and running a business is always a risk, try to minimize your liabilities by only taking out as much as you need. And when you do take on debt, be sure to structure your cash flows so that you are paying it off as quickly as possible. Prioritize debt repayment before you do anything else.

Chapter 7

MARKETING AND GROWTH

1. Perfect your business pitch.

   Have a 30-second speech ready that explains your business as briefly and efficiently as possible, including information about your purpose, your service or products, and your goals. Having a practiced pitch that you can rattle off to anyone can help you in situations where you're trying to make a sale to a customer as well as when you're trying to bring an investor on board. If you can't explain your business in this short time, your business plan needs refining.

2. Earn a reputation for good service.

   Earning a positive reputation is like free advertising; your customers will spread the word about your business to their friends and return frequently. Treat every sale like the success or failure of your business depends on it. Be consistent with every action your company takes and every interaction with customers.

3. Watch your competition closely.

Look to your competitors for ideas, especially when you are starting. Chances are, they're doing something right. If you can figure out what that is, you can implement it in your own business and avoid the trial-and-error it probably went through to get there.

4. Always be looking for growth opportunities.

Once you are established you should be looking for places you can expand. Whether that means moving to a larger storefront, increasing manufacturing space, or opening a new location will depend on your business and goals. Successful business owners realize that one of the primary obstacles to long-term growth is remaining stagnant. Begin thinking of the risk of expansion rather than resting on your laurels at one original location.

5. Diversify your income streams.

Another way to increase the value of your business is by seeking out other areas where you can make money. Assuming you've already established your primary business, look around and see where you could offer a different service or product. Maybe your customers frequently visit your store for one item and immediately go to another store for another item. Find out what that other item is and offer it.

WAYS TO BECOME A MORE SUCCESSFUL ENTREPRENEUR

Owning a business gives you a sense of freedom and empowerment as you watch it grow.

Entrepreneurs make decisions for themselves, realize their creative visions, and develop lasting relationships with other entrepreneurs, customers, and vendors.

It's a great way to live. I've put together these tips to help you become more successful, too.

1. Get Gritty

   Grit is perseverance. Grit is the attitude that we expect of entrepreneurs. Grit is the ability to keep working when everyone tells you to give up. If you want to be a successful entrepreneur, you have to be gritty.

   Honestly, without hard work and perseverance, you're not going anywhere in the entrepreneurial world.

2. To Become a Successful Entrepreneur, You Must Challenge Yourself.

   If you want to be a successful entrepreneur, you have to challenge yourself. No one else will push you, so it's up to you to do it.

   Challenges keep entrepreneurs nimble and on their toes. If you're constantly looking for the next challenge, you'll always be ready for what comes your way.

Consider this example:

You're going to the gym to build your upper body strength. You start doing bicep curls with a 10-pound weight. It feels pretty heavy at first. As you build up your strength, it gets easier.

Would you stop there? No!

Then it's time to do bicep curls with a 20-pound weight. Once you've done bicep curls with a 20-pound weight, going to a 10-pound weight will feel easy. Challenging yourself with difficult tasks will make your other tasks seem even simpler. As an entrepreneur, you always have to look for the next big challenge.

3. Successful Entrepreneurs Are Passionate About Their Work.

If you don't love what you do, don't do it. I truly believe it's as simple as that.

As an entrepreneur, you will need to put in long hours and make sacrifices for your business.

When you're passionate about what you do, putting in the long hours won't feel like a sacrifice anymore.

If you're not passionate about what you do, you're not going to have the motivation to keep going when you're stressed and tired.

Have you ever noticed those entrepreneurs who never seem to get tired? Those entrepreneurs who get that sparkle in their eyes when they talk about what they do? That's passion. If you're passionate about what you do, being an entrepreneur gets just a little bit easier.

4. To Become a Successful Entrepreneur, You Must Take Risks. Humans are generally risk-averse, but part of being an entrepreneur is recognizing the risks you should take.

   Successful entrepreneurs take risks. It's part of the job.

   Successful entrepreneurs also know which risks to take and which they shouldn't. Learn to recognize the risks that will benefit your business and take them.

   Taking risks has a dangerous side, but the opportunities they present far outweigh the potential dangers.

   Learn how to identify which risks are worth taking, and you'll likely become a more successful entrepreneur.

5. Trust Yourself.

   If you don't believe in yourself, who will? Being a successful entrepreneur means that you've learned to listen to your intuition and rely on your wisdom when making decisions. Your ability to trust and believe in yourself will show your confidence. People are more likely to follow and trust confident leaders. Trusting in your own skills will also take some of the pain of uncertainty out of being an entrepreneur. When you feel uncertain, remember how much experience and knowledge you have. Most entrepreneurs start their business after years of experience working for someone else. There's nothing wrong with asking for help when you need it or turning to a mentor for advice, but you also have to learn to trust yourself and your own judgment without input from others. Learn to trust yourself, and you're already starting down the path of entrepreneurial success.

Reduce Fear

Fear stops action. Entrepreneurs have to be able to pivot and quickly take action when they see an opportunity or recognize a mistake. With fear riding on your shoulder, you won't be a successful entrepreneur. As an entrepreneur, if you let fear be your guide, you won't be able to listen to your intuition, you'll be too afraid to take the necessary risk, and your judgment will be clouded by emotion.

If you can find ways to reduce and manage your fear, you'll be a much more successful entrepreneur. Keep in mind that fear has to do with your perspective. For example, studies have shown that the more true crime you consume, the more scared you are of crime.

My favorite tip for managing fear as an entrepreneur is to do confidence-building exercises.

For me, I like to take a few moments at night to think of the decisions I made that day that had a successful outcome.

Thinking each day about the decisions that you made that benefited you, others, or your business will help you to build your confidence and reduce fear.

Successful Entrepreneurs Visualize their Goals

This tip is less abstract than you might think, so bear with me.

When I recommend that entrepreneurs visualize their goals, I don't intend for them to close their eyes and see the goal in front of them.

What I want you to do to visualize your goal is to define it so clearly that it's real and tangible.

For example, which of these is more accomplishable?

1. I want to become a successful entrepreneur.
2. I will become a successful entrepreneur by starting a business that solves a problem for this specific niche of my audience.

The second one, right?

When you can clearly articulate and visualize your goal, it becomes more achievable. You can tell someone, such as a friend or business partner, or take photographs that represent your goal. Go with your strengths.

When you ask a successful entrepreneur what their goal is, they can tell you in great detail what they're working to achieve.

8. Hire Great Partners to Help You Become a Successful Entrepreneur I'll admit that this one might be a bit obvious. Successful entrepreneurs aren't successful in a vacuum. We all have a great team and support network behind us. When I recommend hiring great partners, I don't just mean someone who can do the job you're hiring them to do. You should seek partners who have great character and whom you like and respect.

You and your partners will be working long hours together and making stressful decisions. If you don't respect your partner(s), your team won't last long. Fill your team with people who have great character, and you're well on your way to success. When choosing your partners and team members, always remember that you can teach skills, but you can't teach character.

9. To Become a Successful Entrepreneur, You Must Act Fast.

Talk only delays action. Successful entrepreneurs act

It's easy to get wrapped up in planning, considering potential failures, discussing funding, and talking in meetings with board members. If all you do is talk, you'll get nothing done. At some point, you have to halt the talking and make something happen. Successful Entrepreneurs Spend Time on Important Tasks and Are Patient to See Results.

Do you think that there's such a thing as an overnight success? I recommend that you take a closer look.

Upon examination, the people and businesses that became "overnight sensations and successes" worked hard and long for their achievements.

When you think you've found an overnight success, check and examine the hours, days, and years that went into their success. Please look at their lives, the things they learned, and how often they failed.

Successful entrepreneurs take the time that's required to achieve success. And many of them fail along the way. If you think it's taking too long to find success, give yourself a break. Keep plugging along, putting in the hours, and before long, you'll be a successful entrepreneur. Just imagine looking back at all the hard work and knowing it paid off. Keep that image in your head to motivate you forward through the long, slogging hours.

10. Plan Your Finances

Startups and entrepreneurial businesses need money. It's just a part of the lifestyle. Many entrepreneurs spend too much time looking for money and not enough acting, but that doesn't mean you can leap into the abyss without a plan.

THERE ARE A FEW WAYS YOU CAN FUND YOUR BUSINESS:

1. Self-funding
2. Investors
3. Start Loan

Decide which is best for you, and plan out your finances in the beginning. Try to stick to your budget, but know that the plan will have to be revised along the way.

Who's Your Customer? Successful Entrepreneurs Know the Answer.

One of the most common reasons that entrepreneurial businesses fail is that there isn't a customer.

If you start a business or make a product but don't know who will buy it, that person might not exist.

Before you make a financial plan, raise capital, or even choose a name, make sure that there's a customer who would buy your product or use your services. Without a customer, you don't have a business. Successful entrepreneurs know who their customers and target market are.

➢ Successful Entrepreneurs Listen to complaints

One of the tips I think is most important for entrepreneurs to learn. Your customers' complaints are how you identify your business's weaknesses. Similarly to the last tip, without customers, you can't have a successful business. There's another possible scenario, though.

You might have customers interested in your product or service, but if you don't listen to their complaints, you will soon have no customers.

Take your customers' complaints seriously, treat them with respect, and listen.

➢ Exceed Everyone's Expectations

You're sure to have satisfied customers, investors, and business partners if you deliver more than you promised.

Making promises and not giving is a quick way to lose your business.

➢ Manage Risks to Become a Successful Entrepreneur

Remember when I said that you should take risks? You should, though you shouldn't take every risk that presents itself. Instead, manage your risks. As a successful entrepreneur, you need to learn how to identify which risks to take but also when to assume these risks.

Be sure to recognize where you are in the entrepreneurial cycle when calculating which risks to take.

➢ Read Case Studies

As an entrepreneur, you'll be inundated with your business, needing to take care of it all the time. When you get home and have some leisure time, you might be tempted to read fiction or books for entertainment.

Instead, I encourage you to read case studies. Read the biographies of successful entrepreneurs. Read everything you can get your hands on about those who have already been successful.

There's always something to learn from those who have already done it. I especially think it's essential to learn from the mistakes of others. If you remember their mistakes, you won't have to make them yourself.

Many successful entrepreneurs self-promote or talk about their business too much for fear of sounding like egomaniacs. But if you don't promote your business, who will?

Egotistical self-promotion and self-promotion can be differentiated. Know your business, know some key stats, and have your 15-second elevator pitch polished and ready to go. Then, when someone asks you about your business, you can promote it factually and quickly.

Another way to self-promote without sounding cocky is to know what your customers say about your business. When someone asks how your business is going, you can tell them your customer feedback.

Don't forget to provide some of the bad and the good.

Successful Entrepreneurs Set and Oversee a Positive Company Culture

There may have been a time when company culture wasn't necessary, but with social media and the 24-hour news cycle, your company and employees are constantly scrutinized. Set a positive company culture from day one, and you'll be more likely to work with people you enjoy and who inspire you, as well as attract great customers.

Many entrepreneurs are working with their families, from home, and even across borders. It's essential to know and understand how you want your company culture to look.

➢ Network, Network, Network.

There is no such thing as too much networking (well, unless it's getting in the way of building your business, of course). It would help if you didn't ever stop networking because you never know where your next lead will come from. Chances are, if you network with enough people, you'll bump into another entrepreneur who might have the ideas and connections you need.

You might find a new connection while grabbing a beer at the airport bar; you might meet your next business partner in an elevator on your way to a Meeting, you never know who's sitting next to you on the bus. Meet everyone you come into contact with and have a short chat. You never know who you're sitting next to and what connections or resources they might be able to offer you.

➢ Learn and create.

The successful entrepreneur's mindset is one of learning and creation. As an entrepreneur, you always want to take in new information and create. This mindset can be draining and tiring, but without it, you're not going anywhere.

To stay in the learner and creator mindset, stay away from TV, social media, and movies. These types of entertainment cause us to be passive and take in information.

Pursue everything in moderation, but generally, these activities are time-wasters for entrepreneurs. Limiting your entertainment time is a sacrifice to become a successful entrepreneur.

Instead of watching TV and movies, read case studies and meditate. Take care of your mind and body in constructive, healing ways. It may "feel good" to watch TV, but it's not a rejuvenating way to relax. To be a successful entrepreneur, find relaxing activities that help to restore your learner and creator mindset.

Chapter 8

FUNDING OPTIONS TO RAISE STARTUP CAPITAL FOR YOUR BUSINESS

According to a recent study, over 94% of new businesses fail during their first year of operation. Lack of funding turns out to be one of the most common reasons. Money is the lifeline of any business. The long, detailed yet exciting journey from the idea to a revenue-generating business needs a fuel called capital. That's why, at almost every stage of business, entrepreneurs ask: "How do I finance my startup?"

When you require funding depends mainly on the nature and type of business. But once you have realized the need for fundraising, below are some of the different sources of finance available.

TAYLOR DANIELS

This comprehensive guide lists ten startup funding options that will help you raise capital for your business. Some of these funding options are for Indian companies. However, similar alternatives are available in different countries.

1. Funding your startup business:

    Self-funding, also known as bootstrapping, is effective startup financing, especially when starting your business. First-time entrepreneurs often have trouble getting funding without first showing some traction and a plan for potential success. You can invest from your savings or bring your family and friends to contribute. It will be simple to raise because there will be fewer formalities and compliances, as well as a lower cost of growing. In most situations, family and friends are flexible with the interest rate.

    Self-funding or bootstrapping should be considered the first funding option because of its advantages. When you have your own money, you are linked to the business. At a later stage, investors consider this a good point. But this is suitable only if the initial requirement is small. Some enterprises need money right from the start, and for such companies, bootstrapping may not be a good option.

    Bootstrapping is also about stretching resources—both financial and otherwise—as far as possible.

2. Crowdfunding As A Funding Option:

Crowdfunding is one of the newer ways of funding a startup that has been gaining popularity lately. It's like taking a loan, pre-order, contribution, or investment from more than one person simultaneously. It is how it works with crowdfunding —An entrepreneur will put up a detailed description of his business on a crowdfunding platform. He will mention the goals of his company, plans for making a profit, how much funding he needs and for what reasons, etc., and then consumers can read about the company and give money if they like the idea. Those giving money will make online pledges with the promise of pre-buying the product or donating. Anyone can contribute money toward helping a business that they believe in.

Why you should consider crowdfunding as a funding option for your business:

The best thing about crowdfunding is that it can also generate interest and hence help in marketing the product alongside financing. It is also a boon if you are looking for any demand for the product you are working with. This process can cut out professional investors and brokers by putting funding in the hands of ordinary people. It might also attract venture- capital investment if a company has a successful campaign.

Also, keep in mind that crowdfunding is a competitive place to earn funding, so unless your business is absolutely rock solid and can gain the attention of the average consumer through just a description and some images online, you may not find crowdfunding to work for you in the end.

3. Get Angel Investment In Your Startup:

Angel investors are individuals with surplus cash and a keen interest in investing in upcoming startups. They also work in groups of networks to collectively screen the proposals before investing. They can also offer mentoring or advice alongside capital.

Angel investors have helped start many prominent companies, including Google, Yahoo, and Alibaba. This alternative form of investing typically occurs in a company's early stages of growth, with investors expecting a 30 percent equity return. They prefer to take more risks in investments for higher returns.

Angel investment as a funding option has its shortcomings too. Angel investors invest less than venture capitalists (covered in the next point).

4. Get Venture Capital For Your Business:

This is where you make the big bets. Venture capitalists are professionally managed funds that invest in companies with huge potential. They usually invest in a business against equity and exit when there is an IPO or an acquisition. VCs provide expertise and mentorship and act as a litmus test of where the organization is going, evaluating the business from a sustainability and scalability point of view.

A venture capital investment may be appropriate for small businesses that They are beyond the startup phase and are already generating revenues. Fast-growth companies like Flipkart, Uber, etc., with an exit strategy already in place, can gain up to tens of millions of dollars that can be used to invest, network, and grow their company quickly.

However, there are a few downsides to venture capitalists as a funding option. VCs have a short leash regarding company loyalty and often look to recover their investment within three to five years. If you have a product that is taking longer than that to get to market, then venture-capital investors may not be very interested in you.

They typically look for more considerable opportunities that are a little bit more stable, companies with a strong team of people and good traction. You also have to be flexible with your business and sometimes give up a little bit more control, so if you're not interested in too much mentorship or compromise, this might not be your best option.

5. Get Funding From Business Incubators & Accelerators:

Early-stage businesses can consider Incubator and Accelerator programs as funding options. These programs are launched in almost every major city. They assist hundreds of startup businesses every year.

Though used interchangeably, there are few fundamental differences between the two terms. Incubators are like parents to children, who nurture the business by providing shelter, tools, training, and networking opportunities to a business. Accelerators do more or less the same thing, but an incubator helps/assists/nurtures a company to walk, while an accelerator helps to run/take a giant leap.

These programs usually run for 4–8 months and require a time commitment from the business owners. You will also be able to make good connections with mentors, investors, and other fellow startups using this platform.

6. Raise Funds By Winning Contests:

An increase in the number of contests has tremendously helped to maximize fundraising opportunities. It encourages entrepreneurs with business ideas to set up their businesses. In such competitions, you have to build a product or prepare a business plan. It would help if you made your project stand out to improve your success in these contests. You can either present your idea to someone or pitch it through a business plan. It should be comprehensive enough to convince anyone that your picture is worth investing in.

7. Raise Money Through Bank Loans:

Usually, banks are the first place that entrepreneurs go when thinking about funding.

The bank provides two kinds of financing for businesses. One is a working capital loan, and the other is funding. A working capital loan is required to run one complete cycle of revenue-generating operations, and hypothecating stocks and debtors usually decide the limit. Funding from the bank would involve the usual process of sharing the business plan and the valuation details, along with the project report, based on which the loan is sanctioned.

8. Get Business Loans From Microfinance Providers or NBFCs

What do you do when you can't qualify for a bank loan? There is still an option. Microfinance is access to financial services for those who would not have access to conventional banking services. It is increasingly becoming popular for those whose requirements are limited and whose credit ratings are not favored by banks.

9. Govt Programs That Offer Startup Capital:

To boost innovative product companies, the government has launched a "Bank of ideas and innovations" program. You are supposed to submit your business plan, and once approved, the loan gets sanctioned.

If you comply with the eligibility criteria, government grants as a funding option could be one of the best. It would help if you made yourself aware of the various government initiatives.

10. Quick Ways to Raise Capital for Your Company

There are a few more ways to raise funds for your business. However, these might not work for everyone. Still, check them out if you need quick cash. Product Pre-sale: Selling your products before they are released is an often overlooked but highly effective way to raise funds for your business. Remember how Apple and Samsung started pre-orders of their products well ahead of the official launch? It's a great way to improve cash flow and prepare yourself for consumer demand.

Selling Assets: This might sound like a challenging step, but it can help you meet your short-term fund requirements. Once you overcome the crisis, you can again buy back the assets.

Credit Cards: Business credit cards are among the most readily available ways to finance a startup and can be a quick way to get instant money. If you are a new business and don't have a ton of expenses, you can use a credit card and keep paying the minimum payment. However, keep in mind that the interest rates and costs on the cards can build very quickly, and carrying that debt can be detrimental to a business owner's credit.

THE BEST SMALL BUSINESSES TO INVEST IN

The world of investment offers opportunities that come in many shapes and forms. Small businesses require more work and risk than many other investments, but the payoff can be huge. Small businesses are a significant part of the economy and provide jobs for nearly half of the U.S. workforce. They are also one of the best paths to long-term wealth for you and your family if you choose the right business.

Businesses to Invest In: Once you have a dedicated bank account, it's easy to manage your finances and keep your personal and business finances separate. Here are a few ideas for some of the small businesses you can invest in:

1. Real Estate Sales and Management

   You don't need any specific degree to get into real estate. You can come from any background and hit the books to earn a real estate license in your state. Some may require a specialized broker's license or property manager's license to operate your own real estate office.

   But once you do, it is another business that requires little more than a computer and your time. Much of real estate is about building relationships, creating a regular funnel of new clients, and marketing properties for the fastest possible sale.

   Typical real estate commissions are 6% of the sale price, split between the buyer's and seller's agents. Selling a typical $250,000 home yields a $7,500 payday for each agent. Put together two of those per month, and you'll quickly hit a six-figure income.

2. Accounting

   If you are good with numbers, accounting may be for you. Accounting and related professions require just a license and a computer, depending on your state's requirements. The most common professional designation for an accountant is CPA, or certified public accountant.

More often than not, an accountant will have a degree in accounting, finance, business management, or a related topic. Higher-educated accountants can demand higher rates and provide higher-value services, such as consulting and financial analysis.

3. Copywriting

Someone needs to write the content of every website, large and small. Blog posts, white papers, articles, how-tos, advertisements, guides, and other features require someone with native-level English writing abilities and impeccable grammar and spelling. If you can handle that, a career as a writer may be right for you. Copywriting is another high-margin business, requiring only a computer and your brain to start up and thrive. Do you see a trend here? Low overhead means high-profit margins. This type of business doesn't require a physical office or employees. It doesn't require equipment or machinery beyond a laptop or desktop PC.

4. Personal Training and Fitness

Whether the trend is yoga, Pilates, Zumba, or another workout style, there is a consistent demand for personal training and fitness classes. If you can work with clients one-on-one or drop into a local gym as a freelance instructor, you can bring in good money with few expenses.

Personal training and fitness do not require any specific certification in most cases. However, it does help to have a strong interest in the topic and enough knowledge to help your clients succeed and avoid injury.

5. Cleaning Services

Nobody enjoys scrubbing a bathroom or a kitchen. Some people loathe it so much that they would rather pay someone else to do it. You can work as a cleaner yourself before moving on to hiring staff and outsourcing the actual cleaning.

Most cleaners make around $20–30 per hour. All you need to start is a vacuum and some essential items from a local big-box retailer or supermarket. If you can land a contract with a business customer, you can earn a higher end rate than working with homeowners in most cases.

6. Storage Facilities

Storage facilities require less manual work but more capital. Depending on where you live and invest, real estate property costs can make a storage facility a five-figure investment or a multimillion-dollar deal. Real estate costs much less in Manhattan, Kansas, than in Manhattan, New York, for example.

But storage facilities require almost no training or labor. It would help if you had someone to rent out units, handle basic customer service and property care, and take care of tenant issues like evictions. Mostly, people's stuff sits there, and they pay you for the privilege.

TAYLOR DANIELS

BEST BUSINESS IDEA TO MAKE MONEY?

In the business world, you can make a lucrative idea from any business idea. You must identify what is missing in your locality, advertise your services, and start working. Some of the best entrepreneurs and business owners are responsible for planning, managing, and making the most of their businesses. Problem-solving skills are required to build strategies and relationships to become known as the top entrepreneurship business. They have to Be accountable to themselves so that top-notch quality goods and services are delivered consistently.

To run some of the best entrepreneurial startups, here are some skills you must have: management and planning, relationship management, strategic thinking, communication, accountability, and confidence. An excellent entrepreneurial idea will fail if you do not execute it properly.

Here are some entrepreneurial ideas that could be incredibly successful:

1. Making Handmade Presents

   This is a great business idea for young people with a creative eye. Those individuals who feel like they have an eye for pretty, unique things can start minting money by making homemade presents. There is nothing better than a personalized gift, right?

   This business concept is straightforward because a homemade present can include anything—that's the beauty of it! You can make whatever you think you're good at, whether it is a notebook, quilt, cookies, soaps, soups—you name it. This business can especially become popular during the holidays. Please encourage your children to make some money from their skills. After all, if they are good at something, why not add a little encouragement by introducing the concept of earning money? You never know this could turn out to be the best entrepreneurial startup with little or no startup cost.

2. Gift Wrapping

It sounds pretty ordinary, but it can become one of the top entrepreneurship opportunities. The truth is that some people can not wrap gifts to save their lives. However, others can wrap them so tastefully and beautifully that tearing off the wrapping paper is almost painful. In today's world, gift wrapping has become a real skill. It is a small-scale entrepreneurship business idea with loads of growth potential. The best part is that this is not a seasonal business. Even though there might be a spike during the holiday season, people need gift-wrapping services for birthdays, weddings, housewarmings, and childbirth. Of course, if you want to fall into the most popular entrepreneurship business category, you must step away from the basic foil paper and curly ribbons. Instead, consider hand-painted, customized wrapping paper in pastel and bold colors or wrapping presents in a way that portrays the theme of the present itself. It sounds like a successful entrepreneur's business idea to bring in extra cash flow.

3. Pet-Sitting service

Pet sitting sounds similar to babysitting, right? It is a different entrepreneurship idea that can come in handy. Pet sitting and dog walking is a legitimate worry for many pet owners, especially those who travel for business purposes or those planning a family vacation, about what to do with their pets. Of course, while they are away, the pets still need to be fed, walked, and looked after. This is a simple business idea for an entrepreneur. Teenagers can also opt to do this job as it does not require too much effort or capital. Younger kids are great with pets and animals. They make loving caretakers who can take any pet for a walk every day, feed them, and provide grooming services.

Pet sitting services allow families and individuals to travel in peace, knowing their precious animals will be satisfactorily looked after in their absence. It is also an excellent way to get extra money; as usual, people are desperate for such services and will pay whatever amount as long as they can travel without any stress.

4. Social Marketing

One of the top 10 entrepreneurial ideas is social marketing through social media. In a world where everything is becoming more digitized, social marketing is a good idea for any successful business. It can turn into a booming business for entrepreneurs, especially young entrepreneurs! Youngsters spend most of their time on social media, so why not make some money? Older people are also on social media. You can advertise as a dog walker and get offers from dog owners. Senior citizens with little energy left to take their dogs for walks will happily contact you. If you are looking for an entrepreneurial new business idea, this is it. Encourage young people to create content for a service, cause, or product. Let them search for whatever they feel most passionate about, starting an online business. There's plenty of fish in the sea, so this should not be too difficult. Once they can attract others to their cause, all they need to learn are some primary social media and internet marketing tricks to bring their online business idea to light.

This online business idea will skyrocket as more giant multinationals discover these young entrepreneurs and take them on board to market their products. They will also continue earning passive income from affiliate marketing if they join affiliate programs. When one is using social media, there are endless ways of starting successful businesses.

5. Baking

People love to eat. It is what gets them through the day. If you are looking for a small entrepreneur business idea, baking supplies could be your calling. It doesn't have to be cookies. It can also be cupcakes, pound cakes, zucchini bread, and even savory items like lasagna and spaghetti. This small business idea offers good earning potential, especially since baked goods don't require a lot of effort to make and are easy to transport and sell.

All you need to do is get top-quality ingredients for the lowest price to help reduce your startup costs. Buying them in bulk will help bring down your costs. To limit investment time, the trick is to streamline the production process. Your social media presence will also help you market your products and reach a wider audience. After all, a small entrepreneur's idea can turn into something big one day. For now, young entrepreneurs must learn to manage their studies with a side job.

6. Setting up Devices

If you are tech-savvy and see someone fiddling with their gadgets cluelessly, approach them and offer them your services at affordable rates. Your potential client will most likely agree, and you will be able to earn extra cash.

Have you ever been to an Apple store and felt instantly overwhelmed because you had no idea how to use the devices? You look over to your left, and you see a small child effortlessly scrolling through the phone. Wait, didn't the two of you walk in simultaneously? How does the kid magically know what to do while you can't figure anything out? The youths and children of today are more tech-savvy than adults—yes, it's true. It's almost as if they are born knowing how to download things and make their way from one application to another. This might annoy parents who can never seem to get their kids off specific gadgets. However, this is a skill to master as it can turn into a profitable and excellent entrepreneurial idea. A life coach will help mentor your child and show them how to earn from their talents. Initially, you can look for a prospective client for your business idea by making home calls. With sheer determination and hard work, your enterprise will fall on the list of successful entrepreneur businesses.

7. Creating Local Jewelry

Local jewelry has lately taken the world by storm. It is a unique entrepreneur's business idea with minimal chance of failure. With so many options, ideas, and inspirations available via Pinterest, jewelry designing is among the top 100 business ideas for young entrepreneurs.

Of course, you need to ensure that you look at your target audience and produce pieces that fall within the budget. Even though you want to build a brand name, keeping overpriced jewelry is not a good idea, especially if you start, because it will scare potential clients away. You don't have to make complex jewelry like rings or necklaces. Instead, you can opt for wooden beads, thick ropes, painted glass, and even hemp bracelets. Recently, astrology jewelry has become extremely popular as people become more and more interested in constellations. What better entrepreneur home business idea to have? You can also set up pop-up stalls now and then at local shows or bazaars.

8. Making Gift Baskets

If you're still unsatisfied and are thinking, "What are some good business ideas?" Don't lose hope. We promise that in this article, you will find something that calls out to your interests. One thing that most creative people love doing is organizing, and this idea will fit perfectly for small business owners. If you are someone who loves giving presents to your friends and enjoys collecting different things, making gift baskets may be good for you. To do this, you need to identify what your market wants. However, that's not the only thing. You must also figure out new and unique ways to provide your service. Of course, the contents of the gift basket need to be customizable so that people can choose what to put in it depending on the occasion.

You can also stock up on some pre-made baskets for special occasions, such as birthdays, anniversaries, childbirth, apologies, and even job promotions. As the holiday season approaches, start making baskets for Easter, Mother's Day, Christmas, and New Year's. If you are looking for business ideas to make money, this could be your calling. Many people will happily support a local business with unique gift baskets.

9. Building an Online Presence

You'd be surprised that some small-scale entrepreneurial ideas start from building an online presence. Before you begin to underestimate this, could you give it some thought? Whether you want to become a model for clothes and jewelry, review the best food places in town, or even check the latest gadgets, your options are endless. If you are someone who is social media savvy and has brilliant communication skills, this could be an excellent idea for entrepreneurship.

Many people earn money via YouTube, Facebook, and Instagram. The more followers you have, the more reach you gain. Once you have enough reach and your followers cross the 1K mark, you will start increasing. Soon enough, other businesses will be sending you their products to review and post so that your followers can know about their business. Not only does this encourage other companies to hire you, but it also means you get a bunch of free products. Who wouldn't want that? Your online presence could also help your online working business venture. You could be a virtual assistant to a big or small company and work remotely. You can also be a graphic designer and offer graphic design services remotely for your customers and get extra money.

Another way to earn money online is by offering writing services to your clients as a freelance writer and writing skills. Content marketing is a sought-after skill that will surely offer you extra cash.

All these services have small startup fees if any. A computer and sound, stable internet will help you establish an authoritative online presence while earning extra money.

10. Event Planning

Are you looking for one of the most profitable business ideas? Becoming an event planner Event planners can find business anywhere, any time. All you need are good organizational and communication skills. The truth is that most people are highly dependent on vendors. They wish to hire someone for the most straightforward setup because they do not have the time, creativity, or effort to do the work themselves. But who's complaining? That means more business for you! Event planning can be for birthdays, anniversaries, graduation parties, and, of course, weddings. The best part is that you only need to excel in a handful of setup execution ideas. Most of the time, people don't know what they want. You would have to show them a scrapbook and inspire them with some of your work.

When planning events, try to build a rapport with local vendors. Book them in advance so that you can rely on the same group of vendors each time you need to get an event planned. Coordinating will help save costs and build trust, making your work easier.

11. Photography

Another easy-to-enterprise business that is rapidly growing is photography. It is one of the top business ideas for entrepreneurs due to the sheer demand for photographers in the market. Photography can turn into a brilliant business for someone who enjoys being behind the camera and understands complexities such as how light and background affect a scene.

However, don't be fooled into believing that you can simply pick up a camera and offer photography as a service. Business startups need careful planning. There will be loads of trial and error involved before you learn not to make the same mistakes again.

Angles are especially important when it comes to photography. You can also sign up for an online course to help you navigate through this field. If you are looking to license your work online, you can create an account on Getty Images, iStock, Dreamstime, Flickr, or any of the various photo-sharing platforms that are currently available and get to earn passive income from your photos.

12. Non-Profit Work

The best part about being a child is believing in everything good, pure, magical, and idealistic. Youngsters believe that they can find their place in the world and do anything. Change seems like the easiest thing ever, and most individuals are dying to make a difference in the world. Why should you stop feeling this way as you grow up?

When looking for business ideas for entrepreneurs, one of the things you can opt for is non-profit work. It will encourage you to become part of something you feel deeply and passionately about.

Even though most non-profit businesses operate on donations, you can start your enterprise. Initially, you can start by learning how to allocate resources and funds. Soon enough, you will understand the workings of a non-profit business and will be able to make your contacts in the field and get funding.

13. Creating How-To Videos

Are you a home business entrepreneur looking for something to do on the side while you study or work full-time? If so, one entrepreneur idea that may suit your schedule is creating how-to videos. These are fun to watch and can be extremely engaging.

Many people watch how-to videos whenever they don't understand how to work a device. However, this does not need to be limited to a gadget. How-to videos can exist for literally anything—whether it includes how to brighten dull jewelry or how to prevent your hair from getting damaged while swimming. There are several options you can choose from, depending on where your interests lie.

If you want to stick to a particular hobby, you can create a website and only post how-to videos for that subject. As you start, provide access to your videos for free to people who sign up on your mailing lists. You can also promote some items in the process as an affiliate marketer.

The chances are that soon enough, you will be collaborating with other businesses who want you to create videos for their products, and you will get good money from promoting their services. The only skills you need to have when making how-to videos are being confident in front of the camera, knowing what you are talking about, and using good-quality cameras and correct angles.

14. Art collecting

Art collecting is a successful entrepreneur's small business idea with loads of potential. It is precisely what it sounds like-you collect pieces of art from different places and exhibit them to people now and then. While you add to your collection, you can also alter pieces to throw in your personal touch. Doing this will reflect your personality and add a new spin on products that are not available anywhere else. Personalization helps create exclusivity. As an art collector, you can sell your items at art shows, festivals, flea markets, garage sales, and farmer's markets. Of course, you need to give the original artist credit so that you do not steal their work. Moreover, remember to pay them for their hard work before you recreate their product. This business will give you a good profit margin.

15. Cleaning Service

One of the top 10 entrepreneurial business ideas includes starting a cleaning service. As a child, you must have been to clean your room a dozen times before guests came over to the house. Growing up, you might have become someone who loves cleaning and washes whenever you are stressed out or need to be productive. If this sounds familiar, running a cleaning service could be the job of your dreams.

You can start by providing neighborhood families with cleaning services to help them organize their houses. Your target market should include professionals, families with small children, and working parents. Believe us when we say that they will need your help the most.

This entrepreneurial idea can become highly successful and profitable if you earn a name for yourself. Soon enough, you will start to gain more customers through word of mouth and make loads of money.

OTHER BUSINESS IDEAS

1. Consulting business

   Consulting is a highly profitable business. Digital technologies have caused the change and increased demand for experts with new knowledge. Online marketing makes it much easier to attract clients. Even though you may be a high-level consultant, you should still provide a detailed business plan.

   To know more, start streaming the courses on Business Town that include How to start a business consulting enterprise, LinkedIn profiles that get sales, starting a business 101, How to Create a Business Plan, and many others. Business Town is free for users.

2. Landscaping business

   Landscaping is another perfect small business with many opportunities to increase. It would help if you had a second-hand mower and a grass catcher. Some standard services include leaf collection, yard clean-up, edging, weeding, snowplowing, and fertilizer application. You can make a lot of money from lawn cutting. Even if you can cut down a few lawns yourself, you will probably earn more per hour than most workers do in the real world.

3. Personal Training

   Many people want to stay healthy and fit. They may not have the time to visit the gym or be shy. For this, you can advertise your training services on social media platforms targeting your demographic area. To be the best personal trainer in your area, make sure you are licensed and you can offer these services on your premises or your clients' homes.

4. Drop shipping business

Drop shipping is when you sell a product, generally online, but you can no longer deliver the product or fulfill the offer. Instead, you send the order to a supplier, a wholesaler, or a retailer, and the products are available and delivered to the customer.

5. Amazon Store

About 100,000 people make sales every year using Amazon. While it is relatively easy to set up an Amazon store and start selling some items, it is more challenging to build a sustainable, highly profitable business. Amazon, and elsewhere in Internet commerce, are fiercely competitive. Don't open your stores until you have a business plan in place. Consider digital marketing via your website, social media, email, or online promotion.

6. Start a blog

A blog is an excellent example of entrepreneurship that can be started small but could grow at your rate. Choose an exciting or narrow subject. Let your personality shine and provide specific action advice or a point of view. You should learn basic e-mail advertising methods to get a better Google ranking. Create content that will appeal to your audience, and remember to incorporate affiliate marketing. Social media accounts will help market your blog to your friends, family, and the world.

7. Dog Walking Business

Dog walking is a perfect business for digital marketing. It allows you to find a particular and emotionally engaged target customer. You could target social media and online ad network ads directly to dog owners in that zip code.

Chapter 9

HOW TO ADVANCE YOUR CAREER

Advancement is the upward progression of someone's career. You can grow in your field by moving from an entry-level job to a leadership role with more significant educational requirements and responsibilities. You can also advance by transferring to another occupation.

Why do you need to know how to succeed at work?

If you want a career that offers new challenges and increasing responsibilities, look for a company or field with advancement opportunities. You may eventually become stagnant in a job that lacks growth potential, and dissatisfaction will soon follow.

When considering a new occupation, explore its advancement opportunities. Can you move up after a few years of gaining experience, or will you have to move on? Changing careers is never easy, so many employees are stuck in unsatisfying professions. It's better to know upfront whether professional development opportunities lie ahead.

1. Make a new project request.

If you work in an occupation that offers advancement opportunities, ask for more responsibility. This habit demonstrates your willingness to take on new and challenging projects. It also gives you a chance to prove to your boss that you can handle the added work.

2. Keep an eye out for internal job postings.

Many employers have a company policy to promote. Make a habit of checking the internal job board for advancement opportunities.

Apply for interesting, higher-level positions for which you're qualified. For example, accounting clerks may want to try out for the department's supervisory role.

Be honest with yourself about your abilities, and avoid overstating your skills. Don't sell yourself short, either.

3. Offer assistance

Take advantage of opportunities to chip in and assist your fellow employees actively. This advice also applies to helping your boss. By doing so, you'll demonstrate that you're a team player who's willing to step up when needed without being asked. Being proactive on the job is usually a positive habit. However, there are situations when it can come across negatively. Make it clear that you understand your coworker can do the job and that they may not have the time to devote to it.

4. Seek counsel

Ask someone with more experience for career advancement advice. A mentor can give you helpful pointers, and if you don't already have a mentor, put some effort into establishing that relationship. Objective career advice can motivate you in unexpected ways. Mentors can help you shape realistic professional goals for the next few years and provide constructive criticism.

Talk to experienced people who currently work in the field and ask them: How they have progressed in their careers since they started working and how their entry-level job differs from what they are doing now.

WHAT SHOULD YOU DO AFTER LANDING THE BIG JOB?

Finding a job takes hard work, but the work only gets more challenging once you've landed the big job you wanted. Naturally, you'll be working because of the tasks your job requires you to do. Still, you'll also need to acclimate to the politics, the environment, the culture, the challenges, the opportunities, the people, and all the other variables surrounding your new job. So, besides showing up on time and doing what's asked of you, what else should you do once you land the big job?

TAYLOR DANIELS

1. Learn from Multiple Sources

   Some things to learn are apparent, such as processes, policies, duties, and other simple and expected aspects of the job. However, to adapt quickly enough to become a high performer, you'll need to learn things beyond the basics. Something you won't have is the historical perspective that only comes from experience. Thus, it is wise to sit down and get to know the experienced, high-performers at any organization to gain perspective. You'll learn about the industry, the company culture, who the players are, who to partner with, and so much more from those who have had the opportunity to gain the experience you may not have. Beyond learning from others in your department, take the time to learn about how different departments work together and how the organization is connected by talking to other internal business partners.

2. Examine and assess

   Analyze everything you are learning to determine your priorities. Some aspects of your new job likely require more focus, yet they may be areas with which your experience, knowledge, or strengths are misaligned. might be an area you pay more attention to when learning so you improve more quickly where it matters Most. You may learn that certain team members are essential to partner with, but they may be difficult to get along with, so a strategy may require you to focus on developing rapport. Analyze the information you get from your learning phase and assess your priorities so you focus on the right things at the right time. It is never a linear process but rather an iterative process that is continuous and constantly changing.

3. Getting a Second Opinion

   While you are learning, analyzing the data, and making your assessments, you may start to formulate a firm idea of what you should accomplish in the first few weeks or months, but you should get a second opinion. Ask your supervisor what is expected of you in the first three months, six months, and year. The best way to know what your job duties are is to ask and be sure to get clear answers. What specific and measurable goals should be accomplished, by what time, and what are the key performance indicators to monitor to know you are on track? Ask your supervisor but also consider asking other relevant sources who can give you good information, such as colleagues in the same role who have a solid understanding of their priorities and objectives. You can't be successful in a new job unless you know what success looks like, and asking the right people will take the guessing out of the equation.

4. Establish Goals and Make a Plan

   Once you gain a solid understanding of your role, your priorities, the expectations placed upon you, how success is defined, and the key performance indicators to monitor, you have what you need to set goals and make a plan. Take what you know and write down your goals in a prioritized list. Indicate the benchmarks expected of you for each purpose, as well as your criteria to exceed expectations. Try sticking to at least three goals and no more than five. Write your plan on what you will do to accomplish each of your dreams by the personal milestones you've indicated. If you need to, pin it up in your office, but writing your goals, benchmarks, and plans to achieve them is the best way to keep you focused on making a big splash once you start a new job.

THERE ARE THINGS YOU CAN DO TODAY TO IMPROVE YOUR CAREER.

- Set small goals
- Stretch yourself
- Get feedback
- Curate your work
- Be curious about your industry
- Read
- Network
- Get a mentor
- Listen

1. Set small goals regularly.

When it comes to annual reviews, there is so much focus on goals for the year. A year is a long time—too long, to set tangible, achievable goals. Therefore, it is far wiser to set smaller goals throughout the year. Think about your day-to-day work. What could you be doing to improve that work? And then, once you've selected the plans, give yourself a deadline to have learned these things.

2. Stretch Yourself

    The smartest of us say that success is just outside of our comfort zone. So, it would help if you stretched beyond your area of expertise. Do something that scares you. Don't like public speaking? Start signing up for presentations at work or networking events.

3. Obtain Feedback: While self-assessment is critical, it is also important to get feedback. And it's essential to get feedback all the time.

    For example, at the end of every meeting I lead, I ask the following questions:

    "What worked for you?"

    "What would make it even better if?"

    You can learn a lot from these two questions. So much about your work product and performance can be gleaned from these two questions. Give it a try and see what you learn.

4. Maintain Your Work Image

    Do you know how many amazing things you've done this year? Probably not, because you aren't curating that great work anywhere to revisit it. There are countless places for you to store this work in the cloud.

5. Be Curious About Your Industry

   Spend time every week as a student of your industry or company. Ask questions of those around you. Ask your manager and co-workers questions. Ask your company's customers how they feel.

6. Read:

   Spend time reading blogs of all sizes. Spend time reading books about your profession. Read business books that stretch your thinking. At the end of the day, read

7. Network Brilliantly

   Never, ever, ever send a standard LinkedIn invite. Ever. We cannot stress this enough. Personalize the message and tell the recipient what you have in common and how you'd like to help them.

8. Get a Mentor: Mentors are great resources for all these elements.

   Need feedback? Ask your mentor. Need to bounce off industry or company insights? Looking for ways to stretch? Mentor!

9. ABL (Always Be Listening)

Even if you are pleased in your current role, it never hurts to listen to other opportunities and build relationships with new people in the industry. That's what you're supposed to do if you want to grow and improve your career.

Improve your career today by following the tips above! Remember: if you want to win, you've got to work it daily.

CAREER ADVANCEMENT OPPORTUNITIES

What Is Career Advancement?

Career advancement is how professionals across industries use their skill sets and determination to achieve new career goals and more challenging job opportunities. Some companies offer career advancement programs that allow existing employees to move up within the company.

WHY IS CAREER ADVANCEMENT IMPORTANT?

Career advancement is essential for several reasons. Here are a few examples of how career advancement can benefit you:

1. Prevent mediocrity and job dissatisfaction by leading you to take on additional roles and responsibilities within your existing company or with a new employer. For example, consider a sales representative who starts getting bored easily at work. When they get a sales management position, their motivation for the job returns.
2. Create an opportunity to pursue other career interests by encouraging you to continue pursuing your dreams and seek out new opportunities. For example, if you work as a buyer for a clothing retailer and use your knowledge of

trends and manufacturer relations to open your clothing boutique, you create your own opportunity to advance.
3. Allow for increased salary expectations and livelihood due to continue pushing yourself to be better and go after more responsibilities with a higher pay grade. For example, as an entry-level accountant, you make an average of $45,000 per year. Ten years later, you could make $100,000 per year working as a senior accountant for a multinational corporation.
4. Encourage continuous learning and professional development because you may need additional degrees or certifications to pursue a more senior position or role. For example, an IT sales representative can get a job as a full-stack developer after achieving certifications in front-end, back-end, and full-stack web development.

HOW TO OVERCOME CAREER ADVANCEMENT CHALLENGES

Here are five steps to help you overcome challenges and achieve your career advancement goals:

1. Build your confidence

The time you spend worrying about not being good enough or experienced enough for a higher position could be the time you spend taking on a new role and learning how to thrive. Therefore, you should try to build your confidence to overcome career advancement barriers. You can build your confidence by taking a certification course, asking to take on a more challenging project at work, or going back to school to earn your associate's, bachelor's, or master's degrees.

2. Assess your company's advancement opportunities

If you like the company, you work for but are beginning to feel like your job position doesn't interest or challenge you, review the types of career advancement opportunities available. Your HR department may be able to give you insights about potential job openings or help you get entry to a certification program within your field.

Also, assess whether you've witnessed those in your role or similar positions gain more senior roles over time. If your company doesn't always go with inside hires, or you've tried to get a more senior job before and haven't succeeded, it might be time to look for external opportunities at other companies.

3. Meet with your manager to determine advancement opportunities

Another way you can potentially overcome career advancement challenges is by You meet with your manager or employer to voice your desire for new tasks or roles. They may be able to help you take the next step in your career within the company. If they mention a lack of opportunities, consider looking for other job opportunities.

4. Enlist the help of a career counselor.

If you're unsure of where to start when it comes to advancing your career, hire a career counselor. These professionals can help you revamp your resume, identify your goals, and highlight what's holding you back from achieving those goals and how to move forward. Most of all, they have you accountable for your efforts to attain new roles and opportunities.

5. Make use of your professional communication channels

There are a few professional social media sites that enable you to showcase your work and expertise while engaging with those in your industry. You could even create your website or online portfolio. You can connect with previous and current coworkers and those in roles you want to pursue. Your ability to create a large pool of connections within your field could lead to learning about a new job opening or being reached out to by an employer.

HOW TO ADVANCE IN YOUR CAREER

Review these five steps to determine a plan of action to take the next step in your career:

1. Define your end-goal

> Starting your career advancement path by identifying your ultimate career goals can help you create a tangible plan for the future. For example, if you want to Become the CEO of a company one day; you may determine that you need work experience by progressing through the following roles:

- Sales representative
- Account manager
- Director of sales
- General manager
- Operations manager
- Business developer
- Business analyst
- Chief executive officer (CEO)

2. Create a timeline to achieve your end-goal

Including milestones to celebrate as you strive to achieve your end goal can give you something to look forward to, provide a sense of direction and revive your motivation for your job. For example, if you want to work your way up from a server to a restaurant manager, you may determine the following goal to help you gain more responsibility:

S: Get a server's position at a restaurant chain.

M: Positive feedback, increased hostess shifts, and responsibilities will determine your progress.

A: Always be punctual and willing to fill in. Ask to shadow a server and apply for server positions.

R: Work hard and strive to do well to apply for and earn a server position at the restaurant chain to advance to a restaurant manager position later.

T: Obtain a server position one year from today.

3. Take performance reviews seriously

Performance reviews allow you to determine what you should keep doing and what you need to improve to meet your current job requirements. Performance reviews may also help you highlight what skills you need; performance reviews can help you revise old habits and strive for excellence, which prepares you for success in more advanced positions.

For instance, consider a junior graphic designer who used their performance review to determine how they could improve as a digital marketing professional. From this, they drafted a list of areas to work on:

- Meeting deadlines to appease clients
- Asking questions to clarify marketing campaign projects
- Getting more knowledge in Adobe Dreamweaver and Illustrator to improve the quality of web designs.

4. Rely on yourself to achieve career advancement, not your employer.

If you're waiting for an employer to take note of your work and provide you with a promotion, you might not get promoted as quickly as you want to because your employer might expect you to approach them about your needs or assume you're satisfied with where you are. They may also be so busy that they don't look closely at who is outperforming others and deserves a promotion.

One example is if an IT specialist thinks an employer is overlooking them for software developer promotions. In contrast, in reality, their coworkers have taken the initiative to talk with the manager about their career aspirations within the department.

5. Understand when it's time to move on.

   Another important consideration when trying to advance your career is knowing when to move on from a particular job title to pursue a more advanced role. If you've worked in the same position for a few years and you still enjoy your job and feel like there is more to learn, you may not want to move on yet when compared with someone who doesn't get excited by their job anymore.

   For example, consider someone who has worked as an ER nurse for over three years. Although each day brings challenges and unique cases, they've always wanted to enter operating room (OR) nursing, assisting surgeons with more challenging procedures. Their longing to pursue something else may signify that it's time to earn OR certification and look to change specialties.

What is the most accessible business to start?

The most accessible business to start requires little to no financial investment upfront, nor should it require extensive training to learn the trade. One of the most accessible types of new businesses to launch is a dropshipping company. Dropshipping requires no inventory management, saving you the hassle of buying, storing, and tracking stock. Instead, another company will fulfill your customers' orders at your behest. This company will manage the inventory, package goods, and ship your business orders. To start, you can create an online store by selecting curated products from the catalog available through partners.

WHEN IS IT BEST TO START YOUR BUSINESS?

It is never too late to start a successful business. Whether you are a young adult looking to do something on your own or someone who wants to quit their job and start a gig, there are great business ideas for entrepreneurs you can choose from. From being a freelancer who is a social media manager to being a graphic designer or a personal chef, you need the right attitude, business plan, or business model.

There are many profitable business ideas. However, your attitude, perseverance, and hard work will make you succeed. Many small businesses have become big companies, and your business plan may be the next big thing. Remember, most people start as freelancers, but this does not mean they cannot eventually become business owners. The best way to find your calling is to leverage your hidden talents and make a profit out of them.

Conclusion

As you evolve as a business owner, remember to grow as a human being. Being a life coach will give you or your child the best guidance as regards their talent and keep you up to date with the latest trends. Innovation will help your business reach lengths you may never have imagined. If you stay stuck on one thing, you might be able to keep your old customers, but new customers will find your enterprise redundant. Try to bring in new ideas and reflect on your personality with each business step. Building a brand and a name is just as important as earning money.

If you want to grow fast, you probably need outside sources of capital. If you bootstrap and remain without external funding for too long, you may be unable to take advantage of market opportunities.

While the plethora of lending options may make it easier to get started, responsible business owners should ask themselves how much financial assistance they need.

Now the big question is – how do you prepare your business for fundraising? It's better to start from the beginning with good corporate governance, as it might be hard to go back later and try to exert fiscal discipline. To address these concerns, invest in good accounting software and keep your finances in order. Good luck!

www.ingramcontent.com/pod-product-compliance
Lightning Source LLC
Chambersburg PA
CBHW050001230526
45465CB00003BB/1210